Diary of a Nurse
in South Africa

ALICE BRON

Diary of a Nurse
in South Africa

With the Dutch-Belgian Red Cross
During the Boer War

Alice Bron

LEONAUR

Diary of a Nurse
in South Africa
With the Dutch-Belgian Red Cross
During the Boer War
by Alice Bron

First published under the title
Diary of a Nurse in South Africa

Leonaur is an imprint
of Oakpast Ltd

ISBN: 978-0-85706-252-9 (hardcover)
ISBN: 978-0-85706-251-2 (softcover)

http://www.leonaur.com

Publisher's Notes

In the interests of authenticity, the spellings, grammar and place names
used have been retained from the original editions.

The opinions of the authors represent a view of events in which she
was a participant related from her own perspective,
as such the text is relevant as an historical document.

The views expressed in this book are not necessarily
those of the publisher.

Contents

SINCE THE PUBLICATION
OF THE ENGLISH VERSION OF THIS DIARY,
THE ORIGINAL PUBLISHERS LEARNT THAT
MADAME ALICE BRON'S ASSERTION,
THAT THE *PETIT BLEU*
INSERTED HER LETTERS IN ITS COLUMNS
WHEN THEY WERE PRO-BOER
AND SUPPRESSED THEM
WHEN THEY WERE PRO-ENGLISH,
HAS BEEN CONTRADICTED
IN TWO ARTICLES PUBLISHED
IN THE ISSUES OF THE *PETIT BLEU*
OF FEBRUARY THE 9TH AND 10TH, 1901,
IMMEDIATELY AFTER THE PUBLICATION
OF THE FRENCH VERSION
OF MADAME BRON'S *DIARY*.

Preface

This book is a record of personal impressions written on the spur of the moment. I think it best to give them practically word for word, with all their absence of restraint, and their perhaps too familiar tone, so as to preserve that spontaneity and vigour which an effort of memory, assisted by too brief notes, can never supply. A section of the public may perhaps regret that this book contains no melodrama or exciting stories of adventure, with the author as heroine. I am very sorry, both for the public and myself, but, being a submissive slave to the strict truth, I can only relate facts; and, furthermore, my nature is so defective that the grotesque side of men and things often appeals to me more strongly than the complicated psychology of motives. I do regret, however, that I did not begin my note-book until the 11th February—my dates are often only approximate—though I must have entered upon my duties at Jacobadal about the 20th January.

This is explained by my having sent several letters and articles to a Brussels paper at the urgent request of the editor. I kept no copy of them, and, because they did not agree with preconceived opinions, they were published only in the form of mutilated extracts or imaginative summaries. These prejudiced motives I am ready to condone, inasmuch as they have become so general in the Press; but I wish to clear myself beforehand from the charges of "weathercockism" which will not fail to rear their heads against me.

Owing to this suppression, my disillusion in regard to the Boers will appear less gradual in these pages than it actually was, and thus it is as well for me to say at once that, even when I had gone no further than Lorenzo Marquez, I felt that my enthusiasm was collapsing. My travelling companions experienced the same feeling. To avoid involving certain young gentlemen belonging to the Boer *beau monde*, I will not dwell on this point. Later on I did my best to collect the scattered fragments of my enthusiasm, and to struggle against so rude a shattering of my beliefs, but the reality has never failed to rise up implacably and exclaim, "blind, will you not see? deaf, will you not hear?" Alas!

I wish to anticipate another objection. I may be asked to explain my article in the *Petit Bleu*, extolling the Boers' civilization and amiability, the beauty and elegance of their women, and so on. As a matter of fact, this article was penned when I had been only three days in Pretoria; and, in my laughable ignorance, I took the Dutch colony for Boers! I really beg the public's pardon for such a blunder. It deserves to be called colossal, and I confess it in all humility.

Alice Bron

Biographical Note

The author of the *Diary of a Nurse in South Africa* is the daughter of a Belgian barrister and politician, M. Defré, who acquired considerable reputation in his own country by his pamphlets on Liberal policy. From her earliest years she has devoted herself to works of charity, and in particular to caring for the sick. While still a mere child, she and her brother joined the staff of a private hospital in Brussels, and helped to nurse many of the victims of the Franco-German war. After her marriage to M. Arthur Bron, a prominent manufacturer, she was brought into closer contact than ever with poverty and suffering. Not only did she establish schools and hospitals for the benefit of the workpeople, but she nursed many of the sick in their homes. She also took a prominent part in the Social democratic movement, and her personal experience of the life of the poor greatly strengthened her Socialist convictions. Her influence over the working classes was strikingly manifested during the riots which occurred in the Charleroi district some fifteen years ago.

Although the rioters were looting and burning the neighbouring factories and the houses of their managers, Madame Bron calmly walked out, arm-in-arm with her husband, approached the excited mob, and so calmed the men by her persuasive eloquence, that they withdrew without harming her or inflicting the slightest damage on her husband's property. After her return to Brussels some time afterwards with her husband, her sympathy with the poor and unfortunate at first led her to associate with many prominent Socialists, but she eventually withdrew from the Belgian working-class Socialist party, which she held to be too narrow in its aims, too apt to seek merely political success, and too forgetful of its duty in regard to truly social problems.

From this time she devoted herself with even greater ardour than before to hospital work. She set aside a considerable sum annually for the support of a private hospital, in which she was serving as nurse when the Transvaal war broke out. She joined the staff of the ambulance sent out by the Dutch and Belgian Red Cross associations, and remained in South Africa until the summer of 1900, when she was recalled to Belgium by a telegram announcing the sudden death of her husband. Barely allowing herself time to settle her affairs, she returned, as a nursing sister in the English service, to the Cape, where, at the time of publication (May, 1901), she still remains.

CHAPTER 1

On Duty at Jacobsdal

February 11.—I have just written you that a battle will probably be fought here, and that a great many women and children are leaving. If there really is a fight—we hear a different story every quarter of an hour—I shall be able to make only very rapid notes. Sixty Boers, with a Maxim, have just gone past, about fifty yards away from the hospital. All clustered together on horseback, with their big hats and unkempt beards, they make fine figures. The Boers are extraordinary horsemen, riding bareback at eight years of age, and developing into so many chase-loving *centaurs*. Their whole existence, in fact, is made up of riding and hunting, for their land is wretchedly tilled.

Away the group filed in the fading daylight, under a sky swollen with storms, and gradually they melted into the great dusty desert that spreads out on every side. Dimly I saw them jump off at the water, to let their horses drink. As they started again they struck up a very slow, soft, and infinitely sad chant, very grand and captivating in such surroundings.

How strange the sky looks when one of the brief but violent storms, now of almost daily recurrence, is brewing! The clouds seem to shower great loads of grey dust on to the roads. When the sunshine breaks through, it turns the dust into a silvery powder that quivers and dances like millions of imperceptible insects.

No Date.—Fighting is going on at Namdam. We can hear dull sounds of artillery-firing, and sometimes the smoke is visible. The guns are said to be "African," [1]

The varying behaviour of our men is very curious to watch. Yesterday, when the English were considered sure to come, there was the

---

1. This is a specimen of the fertility of the Boer imagination, which is equalled only by the imperturbability wherewith they spin their phenomenal yarns.

greatest anxiety and alarm at the prospect of being made prisoner, taken to the Cape, and maltreated. I do not profess to say whether there is any cause for these fears; I have been told facts which show that the enemy was perfectly humane on many occasions.

This morning, I having said that cannon-smoke could be seen, there was something like a miracle in the hospital; several patients managed to walk to the door unaided, and I had to drag one of them, who, clinging to my neck and waist, succeeded in reaching the spot whence the smoke was visible. Was it fear or mere curiosity? I do not know.

From information I have picked up, and some exceptionally clear explanations given me by a Boer visiting the hospital, it appears that something big is in preparation near us. The plan is of remarkable simplicity, and seems sure to succeed, especially if the English keep to their usual routine strategy without paying any attention to that of the Boers (who, I note *en passant* , have a wholesome respect for the English artillery). I believe the principles of the Boer tactics have been more than once set forth in the European Press. As described by the Boers themselves, their method is as follows: The English are carefully drawn up in line, their officer struts about, waves his sword, and gives the word to fire. Meanwhile the Boers have thrown themselves flat on their stomachs amongst the brush-wood or behind the rocks, and when the English bullets have passed over them the Boers raise themselves slightly, bring the rifle to the shoulder, fire almost without aiming, and kill their man.

As soon as the enemy has suffered sufficient loss, the Boers jump on their horses and fly like the wind. They tell me that one of their greatest pleasures is to mark an English officer, and bring him down. They talk much of the prowess of one of their number, who shot an officer just as he was about to give the word to fire. An allusion to this happy hit sent a roar of laughter through the ward. It disturbed and hurt me.

"Don't laugh," I said; "it's not right. Remember that those English soldiers have mothers, wives, and children, and though they are paid to risk their lives, many of them are doing it to save those dear to them from poverty. You don't know what it is to be hungry, or what the poor have to endure in Europe. Fight if you must, but don't laugh."

A few—very few— seemed touched; others looked at me with suspicion in their eyes; but the majority showed absolute indifference, and continued to chuckle over this excellent joke at the English of-

14

ficer's expense. The Boers are not ill-natured, and these men were simply actuated by stupidity and the kind of pride a sportsman feels in his exploits. The war is, in fact, sport for the Boers, and is their form of pigeon-shooting. The English soldier, alas! is in as great danger here as the poor little birds set free to fly so that very skilful and very cruel gentlemen can pick them off comfortably.

Yes, fighting is certainly going on in the distance, though the heat is at its worst. I am told that it has seldom been so frightfully hot here as it is now, although the temperatures in the Orange Free State are more extreme than in the Transvaal. Even those who have spent all their lives here are overcome. Cases of illness are beginning to occur in the neighbourhood, and we are threatened with an epidemic of typhoid fever.

Now that the patients are doing better I am no longer obliged to wait till my turn of night-duty to jot down my notes. I am now writing in full view of my sick and wounded Boers. It worries them considerably. They say to me, "*Zuster*, you'll make yourself ill if you write so much." I look at them in amazement. I have everything on my hands now, one of the nurses having been discharged, while the other is struggling against incipient typhus, so that I am on duty practically twelve hours at a stretch, with hardly time to sit down. This the Boers think nothing of, but half an hour's writing appears to them in the light of labour beyond the strength of woman. Is this because my writing is of no benefit to them? Now that I am beginning to know them, alas I only too well, I think it is. Pity? No. Egotism? Yes.

The behaviour of the Boer wives towards us nurses is equally strange. Many of them, who have come from great distances, are allowed to stay a few days with their husbands. Some adore us on bended knees, so to speak, and watch us with grateful and affectionate eyes as we tend their dear ones. Others—the majority—look sourly at us, criticize everything, and do not even say "Good day," in spite of our patience with their squalling children, who get in our way. These women, I suppose, are jealous—a very human and understandable feeling; but they and their husbands would be vastly worse off if they had to do with leas indulgent nurses, who might easily take offence. And what an absence of restraint, what a want of the most ordinary decency there is in many of these Boer women!

One of my patients has just interrupted me. With the help of a thermometer and a bottle he has been explaining the direction of the fire from the various guns, their range in relation to their position, and the movements of a Maxim in action. His description was very good. When the talk is of fighting, the stupidest show intelligence and the sleepiest develop animation. The subject never fails to awaken the animal instinct, with all its keenness, ferocity, and cunning.

This evening long lines of fire are seen on the horizon. The English, say our men, have set fire to the reeds on the banks of the Red River.

"How can you believe that?" I ask. "Isn't it much more likely that the reeds have caught fire spontaneously, as they often do after such intense heat?"

"The English are there," repeated a patient, doggedly.

"You are not so idiotic as all that, my friend," I thought, and added aloud—

"For goodness' sake, think a moment. It doesn't matter to me whether they or the sun set fire to the reeds; but why should the English do it? They are not attacked in the rear, are they?"

"No."

"Very well, then," I continued. "Don't you think they are hot enough already without wanting a furnace with them, to say nothing of the risk of being caught in the flames?"

My Boers replied with a laugh—their usual resource when the conversation wanders from their own wonderful exploits. The Dutch regard the Boers as the Gascons of Africa, and tell very funny stories of their "exaggerations," as Daudet would say.

Some able-bodied Boers coming in with news that the enemy appeared to be moving on Bloemfontein, I took the opportunity of reminding them of conversations I had had with them some time before. Ever since my arrival I had heard the Boers extolling their own courage, and saying the English were afraid. As I invariably prefer to form my own opinion, to which end I ask a great many questions, I ascertained, when I reached Jacobsdal, that the English had not moved for two months.

"Why don't they come on?" I asked.

"Because they are afraid," was the reply.

This struck me as strange; but I was then in the first flush of my admiration for the Boers. My enthusiastic imagination adorned them with all the wonderful virtues it had fattened on in Europe, and I believed the explanation. The veil of delusion before my eyes, however, was very soon torn off, and I saw clearly. I cannot say the light dazzled me, for what I beheld was very ugly and very unpleasing; hideous creatures crawling in the dark—lies. Then I said—

"You tell me the English are afraid, and that is why they don't come on?"

"Yes."

"Very good. Didn't they come to Africa to make war?"

"Yes."

"Just so. If they came here to make war, they cannot be afraid, and one of these days they will advance. In that case, how will your little *laager* of fifty men defend the place?"

"Oh, they'll never attack Jacobsdal; they'll go round it."

"Did they tell you so?"

No answer.

"I don't know anything about war," I continued, "but if I were in your place I should look out."

"There's no danger," I was again assured.[2]

I have just reminded my friends of these conversations, and after hearing their news, I said—

"Well, who was right? A silly nurse like me or very clever people like you? It's easy enough to see why the English kept quiet. They were waiting for a general, and Lord Roberts has come. They were also waiting for horses, forage, and ammunition, which they have now received, and they are moving forward. What's the use of your scouts, who are supposed to be so well informed?"

"But, *Zuster*——"

"Yes," I concluded, "you are in for something unpleasant."

Their self-conceit vanished, and they collapsed.

Three o'clock in the Afternoon.—The enemy has been sighted, and will be here in less than an hour. We have just been ordered to hoist our Red Cross flag where it can be better seen. I don't know whether Commandant Lubbe will arrive in time to stop the enemy, or whether

---

2. This is a specimen of the stupid conceit and self-confidence which proved the Boers' ruin. Jacobsdal, in fact, was the beginning of their collapse. They had made up their minds to stop the enemy's progress at this particular spot, and they obstinately held to their idea. When Colonel de Villebois-Mareuil moved heaven and earth to make Cronje see the position in its true light, and when others more clear-sighted than himself dinned into his ears that the English were coming, Cronje replied, "If they are going to be here, so am I." Four thousand three hundred prisoners have paid the penalty of this foolishness, and innumerable lives have been sacrificed to Cronje's vanity. Let his country judge him, and let posterity assign him his place in history, but for my part I think St. Helena was far too great an honour for such a fellow.

we shall be surrounded and taken. I am alone with my patients, except for two Boer attendants, in this poor little Kaffir church, this pariahs' temple, quite apart and a long way from the other hospitals in the centre of the town.

Here I must say a few words about these Boer attendants who have been forced upon me, and to whom I much prefer my Kaffir hospital servants. These Boers are simply men who have put on the Red Cross badge to escape from active service. They do not know even the A B C of sick-nursing, are in a perpetual "blue funk "at the prospect of catching some disease, and are afraid of the corpses, especially at night. I dispense with their services as much as possible, and look after them very closely; but their children and grandchildren will doubtless speak with bated breath of their services, and when a few more generations of humbugs have had their say on the matter, these attendants of mine will doubtless figure in history as so many celestial beings descended from heaven to succour and console a band of heroes upon earth. So be it!

I wonder if I shall be afraid when the enemy come? Perhaps—one cannot be sure of anything; but I think my responsibility as a Sister and the duty of showing a calm front to my patients will strengthen the woman in me. The men are afraid of two things; firstly, that the English will make a clean sweep of the provisions, and that the food-supply will run short; and, secondly, that they will be made prisoners. I tell those who have got up to return to bed. I shall try to pass them as very ill if the doctor is not here. All sorts of wild reports are flying about. Some say the enemy will make all the sick prisoners. According to others, only the convalescents and the Sister will be packed off to the Cape.

Half-past Three.—Now it is another story; the enemy is to leave Jacobsdal on his left, and march towards Kimberley; or, at any rate, try to do so. All these contradictory rumours from outside do some of the patients a great deal of harm, and make them feverish and excited. And this kind of thing cannot be stopped. At first, the able-bodied used to politely ask permission before coming into the ward. Now they march right in, as if the place were a bar. What else can be expected of men who, when they do not happen to approve of the commander under whom they are placed, calmly say, "I am going to join such and such a commando," and go off without exciting any surprise? In battle the Boers choose their own places, and group themselves according to their own convenience. In hospital they insist on doing as they please,

18

and it is impossible to keep the ward quiet and orderly, as it should be. My post is no sinecure.

Wednesday.—An hour and a half's march from here, cannon is still giving tongue. What is going to happen? The fighting-men are, I feel, vaguely afraid of something. They wonder what this forward movement means after two months' inaction. They are threatened with an attack they have never reckoned upon, and are hastily calling in their men and hoping for Cronje's coming. The anxiety is increased by the knowledge that if the Boers are not victorious, and very speedily, the English, who now command the roads, will cut off all supplies and capture the sheep, which constitute our only fresh meat. These sheep, by-the-by, are generally as tough as goats, and stand about as high in the dietetic scale as stewed cat does at home.

Our supply of milk is already running low (thanks to the negligence of the Orange Free State Government). It is terribly hard to have to put the poor patients on short rations of it, and to refuse when they ask for "just a few drops." We nurses and attendants still have a little jam, cocoa, and tea, but the butter, which used to be fresh, has now changed from salt butter into buttered salt. I should think it would be excellent as a laxative.

CHAPTER 2

Bombardment and Fall of Jacobsdal

Eleven a.m.—The English are close at hand; they can be seen with the naked eye.

It is rumoured that, as there are many sick and wounded here—practically the whole of the town has become a hospital—and also a considerable number of women and children, there will be no bombardment. The women have received permission to leave, but many of them prefer to stay. I think they feel it would be cowardly to go while the nurses remain at their posts, the Boer women being, with few exceptions, very brave. We are also told that the Boers will not attack; that an envoy will come with a white flag; that the convalescents are to be sent to the Cape, the sick cared for by the English, and the staff of the ambulances dismissed.[1] Where are we to go?

Noon.—Two hundred and fifty men have arrived—a mere patrol. I had gone to the door to survey the horizon, when two horsemen rode up. They had big slouch hats, and their clothes were of almost the same colour as those worn by a great many Boers. I saw no details, but only the *tout ensemble* of their get-up, and wished them "Good day." The two faces lit up, and two voices cheerfully responded—

"Good afternoon. Sister."

"What!" I exclaimed, "here already? I thought you were a long way off yet."

They told me their men will pass the night here, and that the attack is to take place tomorrow morning. We all complained of the climate, and, one of the soldiers having remarked that it was time the war was ended, in the general interest, I agree with him, and express the hope that we shall all be able to return to Europe before long. They are very polite, and seem happy to have a chat with the Sister. Respect

---

1. Another lie.

for the nurse is, in fact, more general in England than anywhere else, and this respect cannot but increase in time of war, when every man knows that he may need her care. The two soldiers having asked me if my patients were "all right," I replied—

"Would you like to see them?"

They answered in the affirmative, as did the Boers, to whom I put a similar question. I then opened the door. The two Englishmen jumped off their horses, and, holding the bridles, stood in the church doorway and looked at the Boers, whilst the Boers looked at them. It was a scene of intense psychological interest, at first exciting, and then pleasing. The eyes, which might have flashed hate and anger, showed nothing but a little curiosity. Alas! poor food for powder, unfortunate men sent to the carnage, why should you hate one another? Are you not all members of the great world-wide army of victims of circumstances, and is not that a bond of brotherhood?

About thirty Boers have just ridden past at breakneck speed. A few rifle-shots, and then silence. Have the Boers attempted to rescue the few prisoners taken a short time ago? I learn that these prisoners are Kaffirs.

Three o'clock.—A skirmish is going on, about 2500 yards away, the Boers estimate. From the hospital we can see the bullets falling fifty yards in front, and, having gone out to see what was going on, I heard one whistle past me. My patients cried out for me to come back, and declared I should be killed if I did not. When I informed them that in my country could only die once, they seemed to yield to this irrefutable reasoning. As for my attendants, they were a sight. If they go on like this, I shall soon have two more cases of dysentery on my hands. The Kaffirs vanished at the first shot, on the principle that they always have to foot the bill when there is trouble. The Kaffir is the African rabbit.

Wednesday, 11 a.m.—Yesterday five Boers and nineteen Englishmen, including a colonel and a major, were killed or wounded. In the evening I went to the German ambulance to see the English wounded. I said good evening to the colonel, who received me very amiably, and was not in too great pain. As for the major, he was fast asleep and snoring. I asked the colonel what his people were going to do with Jacobsdal, to which he replied that he did not know. Mentally remarked that the answer was suspicious, and retired. How about this for an interview?

One o'clock.—My goodness, things will be getting lively presently! The English are coming along with their guns, which are extending in line on the horizon. I must go and get something to eat in our hut, otherwise I may have to lunch off a fragment of shell. I leave my sick to the care of my wonderful Boer attendants. When I ask them if they are afraid, they indignantly protest. I have my doubts all the same. Whilst I was at my meal, a single cannon-shot was fired. I rushed to the hospital, and met two men panting and wild with fright. One of them had lost his hat. These were my two attendants. The cowards! How delighted my poor patients were to see me! They all spoke at once.

"They've run away and left us! We thought you were not coming. You won't desert us, *Zuster?*"

"What do you take me for?" I replied. "It's all very well for *men* to run away!"

Two o'clock.—I can see the flashes from the guns. This is becoming terrible. The din tells on one's nerves, no matter how hard one tries not to notice it We are so close! The men are pale, and I am too, no doubt. Shells are falling only twenty yards away from the hospital.

"What is to be will be," I say.

"Yes," the men reply. Some make pretexts to call me to them; others read the Bible. Knowing their religious belief, I try to divert their thoughts by telling them to pray. For my own part, I intend to see what goes on, and note down my impressions, this being my baptism of fire. A Maxim has just opened. How strangely it strikes the ear! It made me turn round sharply, imagining that a number of soldiers were hammering on the door with the butts of their rifles. Now there is firing all round us: the boom of the big guns, the rap, rap, rap of the Maxims, and the *psss* of the bullets. I don't like bullets; there is something gruesome and treacherous about them. You can imagine them grinning spitefully at you, and saying, "All right, just wait a minute, and see if I don't catch you." The noise is frightful. It sounds as if everything were being blown up and shells were bursting right in the hospital.

I am beginning to get used to it. Still talking, I climb on a bed to see the distant flashes and watch the shells falling, (I have kept two as souvenirs; they make most uncommon flowerpots.) One of the patients, whose attack of typhus has left him a little "innocent," has begun to sing, to the great alarm of his superstitious comrades.

"Make him be quiet!" they shouted.

"Why?" I replied. "He's like a child, and must not be crossed."

And the "innocent" sang on, with his soft blue eyes fixed on me. He crooned his own favourite Boer song, an infinitely sad and simple ditty, telling of two lovers who meet at last after a long separation, and ending with her death—"*En zig was dood!*" ("And she was dead!") Delivered by such a broken, monotonous voice, itself a mournful plaint, the song was most affecting. Suddenly it stopped; the singer jumped out of his bed into another, and clung to its occupant, exclaiming, "Annie (he called every one by this name, mistaking us for one of his numerous sisters), I won't let the English take me again." The poor fellow had never been made prisoner. I promised to go into captivity with him, and, holding my hand in his, he became calmer.

I felt that I really must go out and see what was happening. I opened the door, but before reaching the threshold I saw a man fall, some distance away, struck by a shell. He, like myself, had come to look on. He was picked up by a German ambulance, and, I hear, had to undergo amputation of the thigh. To calm my patients, I returned to them.

A Quarter-past Three.—The first act is over. It lasted just an hour and a quarter. My two Boer attendants have come back. I asked them if they were not ashamed of themselves. The one flushed and turned away without replying, as if angry and mortified; the other, a good sort of fellow, laughed loudly, and confessed that he had not acted as he ought. He wound up by saying—

"K. was sure we should be killed if we stayed here. He made off to another hospital, and I did the same. Don't be angry, *Zuster.*"

His expression was so frank, he confessed so nicely, and his laugh was so contagious that I myself began to smile, and forgave him. Incidents of this kind are peculiar to Africa; they alone are worth the trouble of coming here.

CHAPTER 3

Entry of the British Troops
into Jacobsdal

A few British soldiers have just come into the hospital after hoisting a white flag in place of the Orange Free State colours, which had been flying on our roof with the Red Cross flag above them.[1] These men are really very polite. After them came an officer with two or three soldiers. He asked—

"Were you not afraid, Sister?"

I looked him straight in the face, and replied, "A good Sister cannot be afraid. She is a soldier."

He smiled very nicely, and bowed, while his men looked approvingly at one another, as if to say, "Pity she's a woman; she might have made a decent soldier."

Next we had a visit from General Wavell, accompanied by his *aide-de-camp*. He went through the ward, stopping at nearly every bed, saying a few words to the patients whom I pointed out as able to speak English, asking them if they needed anything, and were well looked after; and when they replied that they were all right, the general had a kind word for the nurse.

I asked him if it were true that the bombardment was to begin again

1. An English officer having ordered the German flag to be removed from a German ambulance in the centre of Jacobsdal, there was an outbreak of fury and somewhat unseemly language on the part of doctors, attendants, and nurses, who considered their country had been insulted. Another English officer arrived, and replaced the flag. Cries of joy and frantic applause; the Germans imagined they saw the Emperor twisting his moustache and proudly turning up the ends. When will the Red Cross understand that nationality no more exists for an ambulance than it does in the case of a wounded man? The Red Cross and the white flag alone have any right to fly over a hospital, and in time of war we should recognize only two divisions of humanity—those who suffer and those who tend.

24

in the evening. He replied that he really knew nothing about it.

"Let us sleep in peace tonight, general," I said. "We are all tired, and so are your men."

"Indeed?" he rejoined with a smile. "You know that. Sister?"

"Yes; they told me."

And as this answer amused the men, Boers and English began to laugh, forgetting that their respective Governments had decreed that there should be fierce hatred between them.

Friday.—For the last two days I have been unable to make any notes. During these two days and nights I have not even seen my bed; continuous work, interrupted only by visits to the hut to snatch a hurried, scanty meal. Finally, I was compelled to throw myself on my bed, and stay there three hours, with as fine and vigorous an attack of fever as anyone could wish to see—temperature, 103.1. A glass of whisky and some heavy sleep pulled me round, and I resumed my duties. My poor fellow-nurse is growing worse and worse, and I am very much afraid that typhoid will have her in its clutches before many days are over.

Saturday.—There are two hospitals for typhoid cases in Jacobsdal: one, containing sixty beds, is in the Protestant church; the other (mine) is in the Kaffir church, and has only twenty. Some beds being vacant in the larger hospital, those of my patients who were left were transferred there. Two English doctors asked me yesterday if I would take charge of forty cases of fever and slight wounds for one night.

"Willingly," I replied. "Having come here to nurse humanity, and being at liberty, I will do my very best for your men, as I have done for the Boers; but I have only twenty beds."

"That does not matter," I was told. "Put the worst cases in the beds, and the others must lie on the floor; and they will be better off than if they were without shelter."

They arrived the same evening—forty poor fellows, haggard, wretched, and utterly exhausted. With them came some men of the Royal Army Medical Corps, who helped me to put the wounded to bed, and then went away, after asking if I did not want one of them to stay with me.

"Thank you," I replied, "I prefer to do my own work."

And I went on with my arrangements, hunting high and low for anything that would serve as pillows for the patients lying on the beaten earth floor. These forty men, placed under the care of a single nurse,

25

these forty soldiers of the victorious enemy's army, behaved admirably. I did not see the slightest gesture or hear a word that could be considered as equivocal. The men were almost too anxious not to trouble me or ask me for something to drink. They never failed to thank me gratefully and respectfully. It was always "Please, Sister" or "Thanks, Sister." This respect for the nurse is so innate in the Englishman that it remains uppermost, even when the brain is cloudy with drink. During the night I heard a knock at the door, and having opened it, I saw a soldier whose face and one hand were covered with blood.

"I am hurt, Sister," was all he said.

"I see you are," I replied. "Come in."

He did so, baring his head as he crossed the threshold.

The first thing was to wash the wounds, which were covered with a layer of blood and dirt, and then to powder them. The operation was rather long. Thinking it strange that a man should sustain such injuries in the night, I questioned him.

"How did you manage to get hurt like that?"

"I fell out of a waggon, Sister."

"What, at night?"

"Yes, Sister."

"Look me in the face."

He did so sheepishly.

"My man, you've been drinking," I said.

"Yes, Sister; but please excuse it. We've had rations of rum served out to us this evening."

"All right," I said; "but don't drink anymore."

He stood before me, contrite and respectful, as if I were one of his officers.

"And now go to sleep," I said; and, as he still looked uncomfortable, I added, "Don't fall a second time."[2]

No words can convey an adequate description of the extraordinary activity prevailing here. Coming and going are regiments upon regiments of horse, foot, and artillery, convoys of sick and wounded, countless waggons full of stores and drawn either by twenty oxen or sixteen mules, horses, and so on—outspanned in the plain, then harnessed again, and urged on by negroes with long whips that fall heav-

---

2. I had so often heard it said and repeated that the British soldiers are the dregs of London and the scum of the criminal classes, that their conduct astounded me. Since I have token their part people have begun to represent them as "highly educated men." Is there no way to strike the happy medium?

ily on the back of the patient ox and bounding mule. This is indeed war! Close at hand there is a complete contrast. The officers I see in the shops look as if they were on a holiday. Nothing they do conveys any hint of the horrible crisis through which we are passing.

What business have I in the shops? Why, I must try to buy some linen. For the second time here, I have been robbed of everything. To find time to make myself some aprons I am obliged to encroach upon my few hours of sleep; and I have already had to wash my only remaining *chemise* before going to bed, and let it dry during the night. I was tempted to telegraph to Father Kruger for one of his suits; but, not being able to swim, I felt it would be imprudent to plunge into such an immense space. Consequently, I have to find linen here. Jacobsdal linen! She who has not seen that has seen nothing! See Jacobsdal linen, and then die! Still, ugly and ridiculous as it is, I am delighted to have it.

Soldiers, officers, doctors, engineers, all are mentally and physically fatigued. The poor fellows have been on the move for months, but there is no prospect of rest for them. The certainty that the war will go on for a long time yet is staring them in the face.

We of the ambulance corps are prisoners here, inasmuch as we cannot leave the place, but are otherwise free to do as we please. My hospital having been evacuated, the German doctors asked me to join the staff of their typhoid hospital, in which there are both Boer and British sick. I replied that I would do so if no one else could be found, but that I really thought I was entitled to have some more interesting work after having attended so many fever cases. Unfortunately, the German surgical nurses would not give up their positions, which are of some responsibility. I fully understand their feelings, and their refusal does not in any way affect the friendship and the great esteem I have for them. This German ambulance is simply perfection. The doctors and surgeons are first-rate men. The nurses and attendants are competent and educated people. They have turned a church, a school, and a considerable number of private houses into temporary hospitals. They have the electric light in the operating-room, and a special apartment for the Roentgen rays. The instruments and dressings are plentiful, and just what is wanted. This is really an ambulance worthy of the name!

At this point the English doctors asked me if I would attend to about a hundred wounded whom they expected.

"Yes, as far as I am personally concerned," I replied; "but I do not know what I ought to do, or, rather, what I can do. You must remember that I was sent here by the Red Cross from Pretoria at the request of the head surgeon in the Orange Free State service, who wanted a 'first nurse.' At the same time, I have no duties at present, and I am forbidden to leave Jacobsdal. I have already told you that, in my eyes, the wounded have no nationality, but you will agree with me that I ought to ask advice."

"Certainly, Sister," was the reply.

I consulted Dr. Dyer, an Anglo-African doctor, who told me to accept, but added that the German doctors would have to decide whether I suited them. They responded most kindly, and extended their favours so far as to let me arrange the fitting-up. They also promised to give all the surgical supplies I might require. I then told the English doctors that I was at their service.

"Thanks, Sister. And how much a day do you want?"

"Nothing at all," I replied; " but I will ask you for some of your men and one head attendant."

"All right, Sister; you shall have them."

February 25.—The position is rather complicated. I am in a purely English hospital, but belong to a German ambulance, inasmuch as the German doctors have charge of everything here. I take orders from, and work with, English and German doctors, and I feel that there is a little friction. This morning, for instance, one of the English surgeons selected three men who had been shot in the hip or the upper part of the thigh, and instructed me to dress their wounds after the doctors had gone their rounds. These dressings, as the initiated know, are complicated and difficult to do when the patient is in great pain. They are what we call "*spica* of the groin." Just as I finished them, enter the German doctor. I went through the ward again with him, reading out my notes at each bed,

"Very good, Sister," he said. "Now you will please uncover these three wounds."

"Oh, doctor," I urged, "must the patients go through it again? I should never have done these dressings without the English doctor's orders."

"Cut them off, Sister," he replied shortly.

He did not offend me, because I knew him to be an excellent man, and because I always prefer doctors who give their orders promptly. Accordingly, I took up my long curved scissors with their rounded points, and cut away all my elaborate bandages, while the poor patients looked reproachfully at me.

Yes, these things are confusing. But no matter; I am in a position of trust. I have less of the incessant labour I had before; but I am perpetually on the *qui-vive*. Night and day I am summoned to attend to men whose wounds have been hurriedly bound up on the battlefield, and who are brought here like half-slaughtered cattle. As a rule they stay only a few hours here, sometimes a day, very rarely two or three days, before being taken to one of the Jacobsdal hospitals if the case is a serious one, or sent on to Modder River or Cape Town, and thence home, according to the progress they make.

I jot down these incoherent notes whenever I have a few comparatively restful minutes. My mind remains as active as a stationmaster's in holiday time, when the problem of running several trains on the same line has to be solved.

The conduct of all these English officers and soldiers alike is admirable. The attendants are simply perfection. Never have I had, or ever shall have again, such a staff. The only exception to the general harmony is supplied by the men of the Royal Army Medical Corps. Perhaps they think their officers have done me too much honour in giving me such a post; perhaps they regard me as one of the enemy. In any case, some of them, without being in the least degree impolite, show considerable reserve. They are like victors animated by not too friendly sentiments towards the vanquished. It is only a *nuance*; but I note it, as I do everything that comes under my observation.

But now the fierce and terrible animal within me rises up and clamours for his prey. My stomach is hungry, and insists on being fed. The thousands of soldiers who have encamped in or passed through this place have killed all the cows[3] and fowls, so that there are neither eggs nor milk for the hungry typhoid patients. The Orange Free State stores, we are told, have been looted, and little is left.[4] Let us hope that our water will not give out. A regular *simoom* has been blowing for the last week, and thousands of poor, thin horses have to be watered. The food is beginning to be portioned out in a style which enables everyone to realize exactly where his stomach is situated—the sort of

3. General Wavell had forty cows brought here for the hospitals, but the drought was so great that the poor animals could find hardly any pasture.
4. Another calumny! I have made Boers admit that the provisions did not begin to give out because the English had looted the stores, but because the Boers themselves had not taken the trouble to get in sufficient supplies, convinced as they were that the enemy was afraid and would not dare to advance. They get out of the difficulty by lying.

knowledge we could do without; but, at any rate, we have water to drink. We have also enough for washing, which is a blessing, seeing that we live in an atmosphere of blinding, suffocating dust that sometimes looks like a moving wall, and makes us frightfully dirty.

Every day the German attendants show me the widening gap between belt and body. As for me, I could put two women of my present size inside my dress; but I console myself by the thought that Mr. Chamberlain must certainly drink an occasional glass of champagne to the health of the Sisters who tend the soldiers of the Queen.

I say "I console myself because the notion amuses me; but, unfortunately, it does not help to feed me, and I try to forget the present by recalling all the most amusing things I can think of. An inimitable drawing by Cham comes before my mind's eye: three old creatures, a man and two women, on a seat in a public garden, in winter, wearing an expression of such grotesque misery as to excite, not pity, but loud laughter; sitting in front of them an aged, aged dog, looking at them with the same comically wretched expression; underneath, the words, "There's nothing to eat. Suppose we roast Azor?" I ask myself whether I should not roast an Azor if I had one now. I repel the idea, and another rises before me. I imagine I see a certain *chic* restaurant in Brussels, where the fine ladies of the recognized and unrecognized classes, and gentlemen even more *chic* than the restaurant, foregather to eat the succulent dishes which it is good form to declare uneatable. Then my mind wanders off to other restaurants, less smart than the first, but very tempting—especially just now, where fat and greasy citizens gorge themselves with good cheer, and double the delight in summer by doing it outside, so that the poor and hungry can at least have the pleasure of seeing them eat The disgraceful cruelty of such exhibitions appeals to me now more strongly than ever.

While I was walking towards the hospital, some soldiers came up to me, and one of them said—

"Sister, there's a man very bad in one of our waggons. Will you come and see him?"

"Certainly," I answered. "I have a little whisky left, and I will fetch my case."

We threaded our way through the countless ambulance waggons till my guide pointed out the right one. Climbing into the cumbrous vehicle—an exercise at which I have become very expert—I found a poor fellow lying on the hard wooden floor. He was in the last stage of gastroenteritis, and his face was covered with the thick, viscous perspiration that heralds death. Introducing a spatula between his teeth, I separated the clenched jaws, and administered a few drops of whisky; then I wiped his face with my apron and asked him how he felt. The sense of hearing, I have observed, exists until the last, and I advise nurses to speak to the dying, encourage them, and promise them a speedy recovery—a white lie for which there is no cause to blush. As he did not appear to hear me, I took his hands in mine. His fingers contracted feebly, like those of a little, little child, on mine, as if to hold them.

"My poor fellow, you will soon be better," I said.

With an effort—oh, such an effort!—he half-raised his eyelids. All the soul still in the poor dying body shone out through those eyes, already glazed and soon to be closed in death, and thanked me with such deep eloquence! We were greatly moved, and one young soldier could not restrain his tears.

"It will be all over in an hour," I whispered to the dying man's comrades. "I should so like to have him taken to my hospital to die in peace; there is a bed vacant."

"You can if you like, Sister. When the doctor is not here you are the mistress."

"Under ordinary circumstances, yes," I replied; "but I am not free; I am your prisoner."

"What you, Sister?" they protested.

"Not your prisoner, but your officers'. Call one of the doctors."

He came—not in too amiable a frame of mind, the heat being really intolerable—and examined the patient.

"I can do nothing," he said. "The man is doomed."

"Can I take him, doctor?" I asked. "Please let me have him."

"Quite useless, Sister," he replied. "He will have to leave in half an hour with the first convoy."

I was obliged to give way, though, like other nurses, I much desired to attend to the poor fellow until the last, prepare his body for burial, and make him "very handsome," as a poor Boer widow touchingly expressed it when I was about to put her husband in his shroud.

Having failed to obtain permission, I jumped out of the waggon. The soldiers gathered round me, grumbling. It was a shame, they said, to move a patient when it was a certainty that his body would have to be thrown out of the waggon and left to rot on the road. They begged my pardon for troubling me.

"I have done all I could," I said.

31

"Yes, Sister, we know you have; but it's a shame."

"Be quiet," I replied. "The doctor is not a bad fellow; in fact, he is a good man; but you know what poor folks always have to put up with. It's still worse in time of war, so you mustn't mind."

They thanked me again, and I returned to the hospital.

CHAPTER 4

The Treatment of a Transvaal Nurse in the Orange Free State[1]

For twelve hours I have known what it is to be really hungry. It is not at all nice. Vertigo comes on immediately, owing, perhaps, to the atrocious climate and overwork. This experience befell me two days ago. I must premise that when I first came here our hut was used not only as a sleeping-place for the nurses, but as a sort of canteen for the Afrikander attendants. There were three of us women quartered in this hole, in which no foreign ambulance surgeon would have dreamed of putting his nurses, and seven or eight men took their meals in it. The attendance was supplied by a young woman living in the neighbour-hood and by an old negress whom my fellow-nurse from the Orange Free State brought with her. The interior of the place was repulsively dirty, except our so-called bedroom, which the negress kept clean and tidy in a way many European servants would do well to imitate.

In the den that served as a dining-room the fresh meat was dumped on the earthen floor, and left there for days. It answered the purpose of a gymnasium for the mice and reception-room for the ants, which ladies have many visitors, and are not particular in the matter of smells. This meat consequently came on the table rather past the "just right" stage. At other times the meat was cooked immediately after the animal was killed. Goat's flesh at the best is always tough, but what we were given to eat resembled nothing so much as fiddle-strings. Still,

---

1. I make no mention of the greater part of my personal grievances, but I consider it my duty to mention the cruelty with which one of my fellow nurses and myself were treated by the Orange Free State Commissioner. The Geneva Red Cross ought to protest. It is impossible to admit that nurses should be refused food and treated as prisoners. They may not always meet with a conquering enemy generous enough to protect them as we were protected by the English.

33

it was food, and we became accustomed to it, as one can get used to anything, even to eating ants. This last remark entails another story. Returning home in the dark one evening, very hungry, I cut myself a slice of bread, on which I spread the remains of a pot of currant jam. I noticed that the jam was rather sticky, and wondered what new kind of dirt had got into it, but, nevertheless, went on eating until the negress lit a candle. Then, to my horror, I discovered that hundreds of ants had sacrificed their lives to their passion for jam, and that the most favoured among them had found a grave in my hospitable stomach. When I explained the situation to the negress she shrieked and quivered all over with laughter, until I really thought I had been the death of her. Coloured people always give violent and almost tragical expression to their enjoyment.

To return to a less mirthsome subject. As soon as I entered English employment the Boers began to show marked coldness, first to me, and then to my companion, who, born of an Afrikander mother and English father, openly declared her liking for English ways, and, moreover, was a typical Englishwoman in appearance. This coldness was followed by the development of a positive loathing towards us on the part of the two worthy attendants who distinguished themselves so greatly during the bombardment. Their feelings reached such a pitch that they asked to have their canteen removed. The Government Commissioner, who also took his meals at our table, went with the two gentlemen in question, and our supply of provisions was at once cut off. There was no more bread or meat for us, and we were reduced to scraps of biscuit, some jam, and cocoa. My poor comrade, who was now laid up for good, ought to have had broth and milk, and a little bread and meat would have done me no harm, at work night and day as I was. As no food came, I sent for it. Returning from the hospital, I found my companion in a terrible state of excitement. She was flushed with fever, and wept despairingly.

"What on earth has happened?" I asked, greatly alarmed.

"Those disgusting people!" she sobbed.

"What now?"

"The commissioner says, "Tell Sister Alice she had better ask the English for food, as she is working for them.""

"What about yourself?" I asked.

"Not a word of reply did he send," she told me. "My poor brother is fighting for these wretches, I have fallen ill in their service, and yet they refuse me even a drop of milk! I knew well enough they were a bad lot, but I never thought so ill of them as that. Ah, if only the English——"

Here followed loud lamentations.

"Gently, gently," I said. "You will work yourself into a frightful state of fever if you go on like that, and you know I cannot stay with you tonight You may be sure I will find something for you."

"And what about yourself?"

"*Ai corner*" (Kaffir for "Never mind," "No matter," and a great many other things), I answered. "The first thing is to look after you." To make her laugh, I added, "I'll eat some more ants."

All this did me no good, and I began to have attacks of giddiness and severe stomach pains, but my savage pride forbade me to ask either the English or Germans for anything. I can assure you that I was not good for much when I resumed night duty on nothing more substantial than a cup of cocoa and an army biscuit. Nevertheless, I kept up until next evening. Having less work to do, I went to the big typhoid and dysentery hospital to see some of my old patients and go through the wards, as we nurses do when we have time to visit other hospitals. I was standing between two beds, one of which was occupied by a Boer and the other by an English officer, and was talking to the latter when my knees gave way under me, and I caught at the bed to save myself from falling.

"What on earth is the matter, Sister?" he exclaimed.

Before I realized what I was saying, the murder was out.

"I'm hungry," I said.

"What, hungry? Impossible!"

"It isn't impossible," I rejoined, rather testily. "The Government Commissioner says I must get the English to feed me, as I am working for them."

"What!" he exclaimed. "Have they actually dared to refuse food to a nurse?"

"My companion has typhus fever, and they won't even give her a little milk," I replied.

"The scoundrels!" he growled. "What a shame!"

The news caused quite a sensation. The German attendant reported it to his superiors, and the English officer told the chaplain, who repeated it to General Wavell.

Next morning, before seven o'clock, one of the German surgeons. Dr. Kuttner, brought me the last remaining tablet out of the chocolate his mother gave him when he left home. This does not sound very much, but when food was so scarce the act was almost heroic When I reached the hospital, the chaplain's first question was—

"Have you had anything to eat, Sister?"

"Oh yes; I have devoured some chocolate," was my reply.

"The general," he continued, "says you must state how much bread and meat you want every day. The commissioner *must* supply you with food."

"I am not going to ask him again," I said.

"You can do it through your head attendant," he returned. "The Orange Supply Department must look after its hospitals and staff, and the commissioner has no right to refuse. He is not the master here."

I asked the chaplain to visit my sick comrade, and an hour later he came to our hut with a chicken, so that the negress could make some broth for the poor neglected patient.

A storm which the natives declare to be exceptionally violent, even for this part of the world, has just burst over us. I shall never forget the sight. The sky, lurid as in a vision of the Apocalypse, is swathed in inky clouds. The lightning, at first hurled down from heaven to earth in narrow, close-set lines, now spreads out into a sheet of flame, and turns the desert into one vast blaze. Some ox-waggons; and then the gigantic, distorted shadows of a troop of lancers come past, the horses prancing and dolefully whinnying. What a hellish uproar! Hail and rain are falling in streams, that change into moving walls of crystal and mighty diamonds as the light from the sky cuts through them.

Will our poor little hut hold together, I wonder? The storm unnerves my unfortunate companion, and, to please her, I close the door, loath as I am to shut out so grand a sight.

The storm grows apace. The flashes seem to dart into our hut and play all round it. I wish we had some great singer here to give us the incantation from *Valkyrie*. My companion, now lying motionless on her bed, is a tall, handsome woman, and would make the scene all the more impressive.

Goodness! a thunderbolt has fallen quite close to us.

The storm has lasted all night. The thunder has clashed and the lightning has swirled round us incessantly. It was very fine at first, but I began to have enough of it. I did not want to have the *Valkyrie* going on all night; I wanted to sleep.

This morning there has been a calm. Towards noon masses of large black clouds began to form a sort of immense lid over our desert. Small hailstones fell, and in a very short space of time it seemed as if hundreds of Maxim guns were spitting bullets on our zinc roof. The clouds were belching down great hailstones, or rather blocks of ice, the smallest as large as a song-bird's egg, but the majority quite as big as the egg of a pigeon, or even of a small fowl. I could see the English horses rearing and prancing in terror. Many broke their halters and tore away. Our door, fastened only by a latch, gave way before a violent gust, and was torn off its hinges. Wind and hail whirled into our abode. My companion, shaken by the wind and stung by hailstones, shrieked with fright. The negress and I had great difficulty in carrying her into the foul-smelling hole that served as kitchen. As soon as there was a lull I fetched some hailstones for her to suck. She had so often longed for ice, poor thing, that the little lumps of frozen water were as nectar to her burning lips—one more proof that, in this life, everything comes right in the end. An hour afterwards there was no sign of the storm, and the sun was again beating down fiercely upon us. We then noticed a phenomenon which struck me as extraordinary when I saw it for the first time—a *stratum* of condensed air rising to about two feet above the ground. Some English cavalry riding through it looked exactly as if they were in a cinematographic view.

CHAPTER 5

The Coming of the Wounded

The gratitude of my wounded patients is touching. They had heard that "Sister was hungry," and they were all anxious to share their rations with me, poor fellows! Their conduct moved me all the more when I thought of the Boer wounded, who used to look askance at me whenever, not having time to leave the hospital, I made a hasty meal in the ward. If they had only dared, how soon they would have snatched my hard-earned food from me; while the English soldiers, who had confessed to me that, when on active service, they had nothing but army biscuit to eat for days together, were anxious to share with me now that they had better food. Here is my head attendant wanting to know whether I am dissatisfied with him, and what I mean by hiding my troubles from him! He is trying his best to spoil me now, baking rolls for me, and delightedly bringing me coffee when there happens to be any. What balm it was to me, this sweet brotherhood, this goodness of the poor and humble, this exquisite delicacy that exists only in the heart of the people! Never did I appreciate it so highly. And how sorry they were to leave me when their turn came to be taken to other hospitals.

"But you will be much more comfortable," I told them. "This is such a wretched place."

"You are here, though. Sister," said one.

"I would rather be worse off, and have you to look after me. Sister," said another.

"Here's a keepsake for you," said a third, giving me his shoulder-strap with the regimental number. "I hope you won't forget me. Sister."

Was not this an utterance straight from the heart of the people— the childish heart that closes to all who understand it not, but opens so widely to those who seek it? Never, never shall I forget what these men were to me—never!

For a surgical nurse who understands her business, the English doctors are the best possible masters, inasmuch as they leave even the most difficult dressings to her care, and trust her thoroughly in everything relating to the nursing and conveyance of the wounded. The German doctors are just, kind, marvellously skilful, and extremely conscientious. Their constant goodness to me makes up for much that is hard to bear.[1]

How many more of these poor fellows, English and Boers, are to fall? When is this horrible butchery to stop? An English doctor tells me that eight hundred wounded are expected here this evening. Eight hundred! Good heavens!

I waited for the convoy nearly all night, and at daybreak the long line of waggons, with their dismal load of mortality, began to cross the plain. There were six hundred and seventy-three wounded men (according to the official figures), heaped on top of each other, all in need of fresh dressings, but having to wait their turn until the worst cases had been picked out. What a task it was to make this selection under the gaze of those imploring eyes! May Heaven have pity on them, and on me! How wretchedly small and helpless I felt! How I yearned for arms long as Charity, and a bosom as wide as Humanity itself, to clasp them all to me in an outburst of love and grief! They never knew what an anguish of rebellious despair was hidden beneath the Sister's impassive exterior.

When the bulk of the work had been disposed of, the German doctors arrived. They were in a great hurry, but were most devoted, and their skill and knowledge were highly appreciated by the English soldiers. I never told the doctors this, because it might have been construed as flattery, but I must place it on record here. After finishing my work with the Germans, I was able to give my whole attention to the dressings entrusted exclusively to me. For hours the work went on, until the last poor sufferer had been eased, and the last "Thank you, Sister" uttered. Then I went out to see the patients still in the waggons, but I could give nothing but verbal consolation, as it was forbidden to apply any dressings outside the hospital.

---

1. It is my duty and pleasure to thank the foreign medical men—English, Afrikanders, Germans, and Russians—under whom I have served, I belonged to no ambulance, and was thus without protection, but, in this difficult position, I found these gentlemen unerring counsellors, and almost friends.

All the supplies came from the German ambulance, not only for the big surgical hospital, but for mine, and we were compelled to be sparing in our use of bandages and other necessaries. I am afraid the English ambulance is insufficiently provided. In accordance with my orders from the German ambulance surgeon, I was obliged to tell one of the English doctors that I could not allow him to take anything for cases outside the hospital. Nevertheless, he continued to send soldiers for a little of this and a little of that, and I could tell well enough that he was without the proper necessaries. My position was difficult, my pity as a woman and my duty as a nurse urging me in opposite directions. Strict discipline, however, must be observed on active service, and I gave the English doctor to understand that I must obey my superiors, the German doctors, at any cost.

"You are quite right, Sister," he replied, saddened and discouraged, as I was also, by our helplessness.

The look of things outside the hospital was far from encouraging. There were countless waggons with heads, arms, and legs protruding from them. Lying on the ground were forlorn groups and clusters of humanity in khaki uniforms, with blood and matter oozing through their mud-stained bandages; groups of three or four trying to drag themselves along, some carrying their comrades. Among them were men with freshly amputated arms and legs and heads swathed in bandages, from which their faces stared out, swollen and ghastly. Oh, these faces all turned towards the Sister! Oh, these suffering eyes, these infinitely imploring eyes! And oh, the uselessness of all one's longing to ease their pains! Yet I continued my rounds, because it did the poor fellows good even to see a Sister.

How grateful and respectful they all are! I go to the hospital at night without the slightest fear, and when a sentry hears my reply, "Sister," to his challenge, he always humbly begs my pardon.[2] Here is one incident out of a great many. Heavy rain had fallen, and the roads were perfect quagmires. The night was pitch dark, and, finding myself sinking further and further into the mud, I involuntarily exclaimed aloud, "Where on earth am I?" A man's voice replied—

"Sister, give me your hand, put your foot on mine, and jump over to the other side of the road; it's better there."

---

2. In contrast to this I could give instances of the Boers' want of respect for the nurse. I have been asked by Dutch inhabitants themselves to make a formal complaint, but have invariably refused. No one, therefore, can accuse me of attacking the Boers. On the contrary, I spare them—foolishly, perhaps.

"All right," I replied, inwardly admiring this act of politeness. I did as the voice advised, jumped, and walked on with many thanks, while the voice wished me goodnight. I had not even seen the face of this poor private, whose gallantry might put many shame.

Many of my former Boer patients, now convalescent and able to get about, come to see us every morning. They make themselves quite at home, ask for something to eat and drink, complain of being kept on rations at the hospital, and even walk into my companion's room, and sit on the bed.

"None of that, boys," was my remark when I discovered this invasion. "You know very well I won't have my patients annoyed."

"You are so good, *Zuster*."

"You are a pack of Judases," I retorted, laughing. "I forgive you, because you have been ill, but I have uncommonly little to give you."

Smiling and insinuating, they persisted in rummaging the place for anything they could find. British soldiers also came, asking whether they might *buy* bread, or sometimes a cup of hot tea when the rain had soaked them to the skin. We gave it gladly, and our hut became a house of God, where Boers and British mingled in peace and harmony.

Small convoys of English wounded are continually coming in. and I expect three hundred tonight. It may be that these will be the last, and that in future the wounded will be taken direct to the Cape in the ambulance-trains.

How marvellously beautiful is the sky at twilight! On the right, a dome of warm-tinted blue and violet clouds has formed over the English camp. In front, the azure sky, tinged and streaked with mauve, throws up in sharp relief the outlines of countless herds of black cattle with immense white horns, busy ant-like swarms of soldiers, gesticulating negroes, and grey waggons. On the left the plain stretches away into the distant desert, with the little Kaffir church, my beloved hospital, a mere speck upon it. Here the sky, of soft flaxen grey, edged with pink, envelops the arid waste, and seems to soften it with a caress. As night slowly veils the outlines of living creatures and things with her black mantle, a Kaffir chorus, soothing as a lullaby, floats through the air. It consists of endless couplets, sung by two very high voices, accompanied, *mezza voce*, a third lower, by other voices, and sustained by a sort of gentle, far-away murmur from the rest of the singers. The effect is most uncommon and weird in its primitive simplicity.

We have been receiving quite a crowd of officers, who have spent several hours in my hospital, hitherto reserved for the private soldier.

The place is without the slightest pretence at comfort, but they appeared not to notice it. What refined and charming politeness! What quiet but heartfelt thanks, repaying me a thousandfold for any trouble I had taken! There were, however, three exceptions. My attendants gave out the rations at every bed, to officers and soldiers alike. All the officers had sufficient tact to understand that the men who shared their danger ought to share their meals, and they accepted the arrangement. The three young snobs in question refused their food with a disgust that was decidedly out of place, and (they were suffering only from fatigue) in feeble, plaintive voices told their orderlies to prepare some bread and milk, and make some toast; and when the orderly began to spread jam on the toast, they faintly whispered, "Not too sweet." Poor suffering angels!

Such smart gentlemen could evidently entertain no sentiment save a sovereign disdain towards the nurse, whom they regarded as a sort of servant. They took no pains to disguise this feeling, but they were decidedly put out by what occurred when the time came to leave. They saw all their brother officers bow to me with the utmost respect, shake hands with me, and thank me. They heard a field officer say, "We all thank you." What were the poor fellows to do? Shake hands with a Sister? The idea was preposterous. Well, they just sneaked away through an outhouse at the end of the hospital, while I was seeing my wounded out at the main door. I concluded that their conduct was the result of hereditary influences; that, their ancestors having doubtless belonged to the kitchen, they instinctively preferred to leave by the back door. The incident amused me, and I was very glad that the only false note in this harmony of affection and respect was not struck by a soldier. The poor have an innate tact of their own, and we must make allowances for the rich, in view of their misdirected education.[3]

Yesterday the English officers assured me that Cronje had surrendered with 4300 men, and that Kimberley had capitulated after a bombardment. The Boers accept the latter item of news as true, but deny that Cronje has been defeated, although they are already beginning to attack him and load him with all the sins of Israel.

---

3. This remark is of no consequence, but I retain it to show the unprejudiced nature of my daily notes. These three exceptions, moreover, serve to show up, in even greater relief, the fine qualities of the innumerable British soldiers with whom I came in contact. In the same way, the few Boers imbued with generous and humane ideas made the great mass of their compatriots appear even more disappointing than was really the case.

"The beaten are always wrong," I said. "He has done harm enough, without having to answer for the blunders of others; and, now that he is down, it is not for the Boers to reproach him with his blind obstinacy. You have no right to rail at your defeated brethren. Let others judge them."

Those among the Boers who possessed any sense and good-feeling remarked that I was right, but the others persisted in saying it was all Cronje's fault. They were unanimous in assuring me that he had not been captured, that the story had been invented to encourage the British soldiers, that the general in command had received news of quite a different kind,[4] and so on.

March 3.—The news was true enough, seeing that Cronje and the other prisoners passed quite close to this place in the night. The Boers have ceased their denials, but Cronje's capitulation does not seem to depress them at all. They are simply indifferent.

Some English officers have told me an awful thing. More than a hundred and fifty wounded Boers were left on the battlefield, without help or shelter for five days. The English offered to attend to them, but Cronje refused.

"Good heavens!" I exclaimed, "don't tell me that such things can be. Poor, poor creatures! No, I cannot believe it. You have always told me the truth hitherto, but this——"

"It is perfectly true. Sister."[5]

The chaplain, whom I see every day, and whom I take to be a thoroughly upright man, also asserts that this frightful crime has really been perpetrated. I am in despair; I long to set off at once. The chaplain, who reads my thoughts, reminds me that I am indispensable here, and that other wounded are coming. He relieves my anxiety by telling me that the ambulances are at work on the battlefield.

March 4.—Another batch of officers among my wounded, all as refined and charmingly polite as the others. As for the soldiers, I can only repeat what I have already said about them.

Some officers would like to know what I think of the Boers. It is a mischievous question, and he who puts a query of this kind to a woman lays himself open to defeat.

"What do I think of them?" I repeat. "I think I am in their serv-

4. Every time there was a British victory the Boers revived this lie, and repented it to one another, knowing quite well that they were not telling the truth.
5. A few days later I obtained confirmation of the ghastly story from one of the very men whom Cronje had abandoned.

ice."

There is a laugh, and one of the officers says—

"You are perfectly right, Sister, and we beg your pardon."

Then they tell me they cannot understand how a woman can have been separated from her ambulance and left in this desert; to which I reply that I understand their surprise, that I thank them for the interest they are kind enough to take in me, Init that I left my ambulance of my own accord, and can manage very well by myself At the same time, this requires a certain amount of energy, each ambulance being complete in itself, and if I had not been lucky enough to meet with such kind and friendly doctors, I should have had nothing to do here after my several weeks' nursing of typhoid cases.

I greatly desired to join a field hospital, and begged the chaplain to ask General Wavell for permission. The general, accompanied by the chaplain, came to our hut (imagine a French, German, or Belgian general going out of his way for a mere nurse!). In reply to his questions, I told him that I had come out with the Belgian ambulance to attend to the Boers, but that I placed the interests of humanity in general above those of any people in particular, and that one wounded man was the same to me as another, inasmuch as the soldier does not declare war, but is its victim.[6] I added that I had paid my travelling expenses.

"After what you say. Sister," replied the general, "I regard you as perfectly free. I should very much like to do as you desire, in acknowledgment of your services to our people, but Lord Roberts will not have any women on the battlefield. I will not even offer to telegraph to him about it, because I know beforehand what his answer will be. You had better enter a hospital at Modder River or the Cape."

"Many thanks, general," I replied; "but if I cannot join a field hospital, I would rather stay with the Boers."

"Do as you think best," the general replied, heartily shaking my hand. "I am sure it will be right."

General Wavell always treated me, from the very first, with exquisite politeness. Whether in the hospital or the street, he was always the first to greet me. If on horseback he would shout, "Morning, Sister," or "Good afternoon. Sister." The soldiers say he is very fond of the ladies. I know he has a gentleman's respect for a woman, and his pro-

---

6. While on board the steamer, on my way out to South Africa, I expressed these views in a letter to the newspaper which had asked me to send articles, but this portion was never inserted.

tecting kindness and influence—I have spoken to him only three or four times—were very precious to me in my isolation. It is a joy for me to express all the gratitude I feel towards him.

As I am to stay here for the present, the German doctors have asked me to take twenty wounded Boers in my little Kaffir church. I shall probably leave here in about three weeks with the German ambulance for Pretoria, *viâ* the Cape and Lorenzo Marquez.

CHAPTER 6

Departure of the British
From Jacobsdal

Yesterday evening, while the light was fading sadly out of the sky, we heard the merry, youthful sounds of the British army fifes.

March 5.— The last of my wounded have gone. I have said good-bye to my excellent attendants, who have been so devoted to me, who knew so well that the way to please me was to be good to the wounded, and who gave themselves up, body and soul, to their humane task. I have seen the last of them and their affectionate attentions, their respect and their confidence, which they gave me in greater measure than to the doctor himself. My poor hut will no longer be the centre to which, day and night, the sufferings and distress of so many have converged. On this head I could relate many instances of exquisite feeling on the part of these poor soldiers, but such revelations of the inmost soul are too sacred and delicate for publicity. Yes, they are at an end, these nineteen days, so full of labour, but of joy as well, and I must resume my thankless task of nursing patients who understand my position so little.

Well, well, everything has an end, and happiness never lasts long. Other work will come, other interests, other struggles; it matters little to the nurse so long as she can accomplish her task, and satisfy herself that she has striven to the utmost. The religion she follows is so beautiful, so pure, so wide, and so little understood! So few people know how much joy this religion contains, the strength it gives, and how it elevates the believer far above all base envy, hatred, and deceit.

Let me note here the beautiful thought, the Christian faith in the pure acceptation given to it by the Nazarene, which came from the pale lips of a wounded English soldier the other day. We were speaking of Cronje and his four thousand three hundred prisoners.

"Ah, Sister," said he, "I am very glad to hear we have made so many prisoners."

"Why?" I asked, fearing to hear words of hatred.

"Oh," he said, "I was glad to hear it because I knew that they, at least, would be neither killed nor wounded. They will not leave wife and children, neither will they suffer what we are suffering."

Was not this wounded man's pity and tenderness almost superhuman? I was very much touched, and felt myself enveloped in such an atmosphere of real brotherhood that something impelled me towards this man.

"You have a large heart," I said. "Will you shake hands?"

We talked a few moments, and I learnt that he had had no news from England for some time, and was very uneasy. Then he asked me the question which, alas! they so often put to me—

"Am I going to get well?"

"Certainly," I replied.

I always said "Yes" as a matter of course.

Then he continued, "You see, Sister, I ask that because I have a wife and children."

This was the constant anxiety of all the married men—the thought of leaving the mother and children in want; and they suffered still more from this than from their own mangled flesh.

March 6, Morning.—The greater number of the wounded Boers who should have arrived here have been sent in another direction; consequently, there is nothing more for me to do at Jacobsdal, and my little Kaffir church will be put to its proper use.

General Wavell came to my storeroom to say "Goodbye," but I had gone to see some patients. I might have asked him for a pass to go to Bloemfontein. But no, I have not a *sou* left. I have put all my money on my back, and horse-hire is frightfully dear.

March 6, 2 o'clock.—I am certainly in luck. I am to start at four o'clock with an Afrikander ambulance. Oh, joy!

CHAPTER 7

From Jacobsdal to Pretoria
Viâ Bloemfontein

March 10.—We have now been four days on the move. I must take up my story from the 6th. As I was going to the German ambulance I saw that things were very lively in the square. Oxen, horses, mules, and vehicles of every kind were being laden with luggage. I asked what it was all about, and was told that it was the Afrikander ambulance belonging to Dr. Dyer, which had got leave to start. I said to myself, 'I'll go too, even if I have to be tied under one of the waggons."

Upon arriving at the ambulance, I was disappointed to hear that Dr. Dyer, the only person to whom I was known, was to join it *en route*. Nevertheless I made my request. It was received ungraciously enough by an Afrikander (whose exact position I have never been able to discover). He answered vaguely when I asked to see the doctors.

"Ah," I reflected, "you don't know where they are, and when they will be back? I'll find out for myself." And I seated myself on the ground in front of the door.

At last the doctors came I spoke to the one who is Dr. Dyer's assistant, and was explaining the situation to him when the other fellow interfered, but was cut short by the doctor, who said—

"We must find room for the Sister. She has been sent officially from the Red Cross of Pretoria by request of the Bloemfontein Committee. She has done her duty well here, and we ought to help her."

He spoke like a real doctor, only judging the nurse by her capacity and devotion. The other was giving way to that petty spite of which I had already had so much at Jacobsdal. He could not forgive me for having looked after the wounded English as well as the Boer typhoid

48

patients. Oh, humanity!

"A thousand thanks, doctor," I said. "You are kind and just"

He tried to make up for the rudeness of the other by replying that he should be very glad to have me with them.

"You have not much luggage, I hope?"he added.

"Only my large ambulance bag and a valise."

"Splendid," he said, laughing. "Women always have too much luggage."

"And now," he continued, "make haste. I shall send for your things in half an hour."

I went back to my room, and stuffed everything haphazard—even the nests of mice that were frisking about in my boots—into my large bag. The young mice squeaked as I squeezed them in, but I had not time to apologize.

"Then you are going?"said my comrade, who had been convalescent some days. "Well, you are fortunate! I am sorry to lose you, but am glad for your sake. As you will pass my parents' farm, will you tell them to come and fetch me with a spring-cart in eight or ten days?"

"Yes," I replied. "And I can go with my mind at ease. The old black woman loves you as a daughter, and will take care of you. *Adieu*, Sister Emily."

"*Adieu*, Sister Alice."

And we separated, regretting the end of our companionship, but without much emotion on either side, she weakened by illness and I off to other labours, to the unknown, and doubtless to fresh dangers.

I had still time to go and say goodbye to the German ambulance staff. They were kind enough to express regret at my departure, though they envied me. As I was preparing to leave, I stopped to look at some wounded men who were being brought in. Ah, poor things! They were some of the Boers for whom Cronje had rejected the offer of English help. Out of seven now brought in, two had died on the way, and the other five were near their end.

I knelt down between two stretchers, amid the hubbub always caused by the arrival of wounded, and questioned one of the two victims, who seemed able to speak.

"You are from Cronje's *laager*?"

"Yes," he replied.

I did not think it proper to risk inflicting further mental suffering on him by questioning him on Cronje's conduct or the possibility of the Boer general having really committed the crime of which he was accused. I merely asked—

"How long were you left without help?"

"Seven days," he replied.

"Seven!" I exclaimed. "They told me five."

"No, Sister, seven days and seven nights, lying in the open without a drop of water to drink. And it was so cold at night!"

I could not utter a word. I was simply overwhelmed with indignation and pity, but the poor fellow understood my silence, and repeated—

"Yes, Sister, it was so."

Feeling I must say something, I rejoined, "You will be all right here. Cheer up."

He looked at me in a resigned way with his large, soft black eyes, and as the bearers came to take him away I clasped his hand in mine and uttered one of the Boer stock phrases—

"*Alles ter beste*" ("All for the best")—another white lie.

The best thing that could happen to him was to die, and end the agony he had been enduring for nearly a week. His wounds must have been in a frightful state.

Then it was true, after all! Under the mask of heroism, indomitable pride and haughty disdain of the enemy, a general had actually condemned his soldiers to these tortures! He, a man, had inflicted this horrible martyrdom on his fellows! Never had I felt such intense loathing. Never did my moral sense cry out against a more odious and cowardly crime. There could no longer be any doubt about it. The dying Boer had confirmed what the English officer told me. It was true!

I had just time to take a hasty farewell of the last two of my Boer typhoid patients still left in the hospital. The other twenty, who were cured, had been sent away as prisoners of war, and out of these twenty only eight came to say goodbye. The others did not even deign to pay a visit to my fellow-nurse, who had fallen ill in their service. This neglect greatly exasperated her. She was very innocent, poor thing!

At length I reached the ambulance, and we started at four o'clock. We made a brief halt for supper at nine, and I was able to take a good look at those who were to be my close companions for a week, that being about the time required for the journey to Bloemfontein. The caravan consisted of twelve nurses (eight Afrikanders, three Swedes, and myself), about thirty men (doctors, hospital attendants, a Protestant minister, transport service officers, and Government officials, whose duty it was to register the names of dead and wounded Boers and other information), and a crowd of black "boys" employed as drivers. The teams consist of eight, ten, or twelve animals, and there are always two men on the box, one holding the reins and the other wielding an immense whip, which is long enough to reach the leading pair, and is handled with wonderful dexterity by these blacks.

The whole lot of us are conveyed—jammed would be a better word—in nine vehicles, including waggons, waggonettes, and even a broken-down landau that looked as if it were bewailing its hard fate. There was also a truly wonderful mail-coach. No one could possibly have ascertained to what style or epoch in carriage-building this coach belonged; but, the body being painted a bright canary yellow and perched very high on its springs, it created a belief that it might have been planned somewhere about the year 1830. It was like anything you choose to call it, but unlike anything you can imagine. It had a self-satisfied, hilarious look, and its yellow panels formed a most singular background to the heads of the Kaffirs as they bobbed, up and down, nodding and shouting.

Here we all are, crouching round a fire (the weather is becoming cooler), my companions chatting a great deal. Some of the men speak to me, but the women all seem to have swallowed pokers, and examine me furtively from under their white caps. I look back at them, and recognize them. It is too funny! They are not Sisters—that is to say, professionals—but nurses, or, in other words, damsels who love flirtations and adventures and have never cared for anything except their own toilettes. This kind of creature should not be accepted in an ambulance, I think, unless there are no real nurses. Since I have been in Africa, I have almost invariably seen incapables given the preference to women who knew their business. I was so strangely impressed by the disadvantages of this sort of arrangement that one of my first acts on reaching Jacobsdal was to tell the head surgeon that I was ready to take full responsibility, but that I must insist on certain young persons, as ill-bred as they were incompetent, keeping out of the hospital while I was there. My conditions were at once agreed to, and the other two Sisters having followed my example, order was restored.

On the day of the arrival of the big batch of English wounded. Dr. Dyer came to my hospital with five smart, curly-headed nurses, who looked as if they had come out of a band-box.

"Here, Sister Alice," he said, "I have brought you some helpers."

"Much obliged," I hurriedly replied, rushing off to follow the German surgeon round the ward.

This was the first time I had worked with him, and nurses know that every surgeon has his special fads which she must learn, and that he will disdainfully reject the dressing another doctor may have described as the only good one. My attention being thus concentrated on the patients and the directions I was receiving from my superior officer, I did not at first observe what my "helpers "were doing; but, happening to look round, I found they had calmly gone to my big hospital-case and helped themselves, undoing the packets of gauze, lint, and bandages, and opening and mixing everything up.

"What on earth are you doing?" I asked.

"We are preparing the dressings. Sister."

"You have got out enough for a week," I said. "Do you intend to expose all those dressings to the dust and dirt? Leave it to me, and, if you want to be useful, help the attendants to wash the patients."

They pouted indignantly, took themselves off a few minutes later, and I saw no more of them. And they called themselves nurses! For weeks we had performed every kind of service for our twenty-two patients— washing them from head to foot twice and even three times a day, emptying the vessels and cleaning the bedding, and yet the simplest of such duties was too hard for these little humbugs! Now they were having their revenge; they were on their own ground, and took care to let me know it. I did not mind, knowing that it would be all right in a day or two.

After supper we resumed our journey, and, three hours later, we halted for the night. We slept in the vehicles, nearly all of which were simply covered on top and not at the sides. The men lay down in the fields. At the request of the doctor who had received me so well at Jacobsdal, I chummed with the Swedish nurses. I already felt drawn to them, although we had not exchanged a word, and next day we were firm friends.

We have now been four days on our travels. As I foresaw, the Afrikander girls and I get on very well. As for the three Swedish nurses, they and I are inseparable. What good and charming girls they are! Their ages vary from twenty-two to thirty-five; they are single-minded, intelligent, and ladylike, with minds of crystal purity. How we laugh and giggle, we four, like so many schoolgirls, on the slightest provocation! We mess with two Swedish attendants, taking it in turns to fetch wood for our fire and water for our tea and helping ourselves from the fruit-trees of every farm we pass. This is the correct thing in time of war: at least, the Afrikanders say so, and we follow their example. They are very amusing, these Bohemian encampments, by the light of the moon or of a few candles stuck in the ground.

During the day we take our meals lying flat on our stomachs under the waggons, and imagine we are in the shade. The sun is almost hot enough to fry us alive. The nights are pleasant, but are getting decidedly cold. We try to warm ourselves by laughing at all the amusing reminiscences we can muster. We are so very merry that a commanding voice cries from without, "Halloa there, nurses, it's time to go to sleep!" The Swedish girls and I are not submissive. As we are not at a boarding-school we decline to have our hours of sleep fixed for us, and therefore we laugh and talk as long as we have a mind to do so; but as we do not want to annoy the chief, we put our aprons over our heads to stifle the noise, and reduce it to something like the playful yapping of puppies or grunting of little pigs—silly, if you will, but delicious after our long weeks of drudgery.

Yesterday, and today, our olfactory organs have been grievously offended, to put it in elevated language. In other words, there is an appalling stench, far worse than anything I ever met with in a hospital. The road is strewn with dead horses, mules, and oxen that have fallen through exhaustion or inanition. The first few of these carcases were rather alarming; the proportions of bodies and limbs seemed to have been altered in some mysterious way. They lay on back or side, with legs stretched out straight and stiff, bodies swollen like immense bladders, and heads expressing almost human suffering. By degrees we become accustomed to these sights, and take no further notice of them, except to remark on their increasing number. Many of these carcases are in a state of putrefaction, and lie in pools of black, slimy liquid, covered with thousands of flies, Still, when mealtime comes round, all this carrion does not interfere with our appetites in the least. Our low, animal nature is callously and lamentably indifferent. But a truce to philosophizing. We shall; soon be hard at work again, and, in the mean time, let us be gay while we may, remembering that laughter is the special privilege of man.

Brandely's Farm.—Here we are, close to the British camp, with only the road between it and our halting-place, where we shall have to stay at least twenty-four hours. The troops are those that left Jacobsdal a little before us, and we soon see General Wavell coming up to shake hands with all the nurses.

"You see I have come to protect you," he said.

We smiled and bowed, and I thought, "I know your soldiers too well, general; we don't need any protection." Then it flashed upon me that he had not given me permission to leave Jacobsdal, and that he might wonder what I was doing here; but he maintained his usual kind demeanour towards me, and asked no questions, for which I was extremely thankful.

The next twenty-four hours were restful, delightful, and full of unexpected glimpses of Afrikander psychology—so unexpected, in fact, that we Europeans, the Swedish nurses and I, could hardly believe our eyes and ears. Extremely cordial relations were immediately established between the English staff and the heads of the Afrikander ambulance, as well as between some of the officers and the nurses. Regular flirtations sprang up. Several times a day the staff, and especially the general, crossed the road, and came to chat with the ambulance surgeons. The officers preferred feminine society. The Swedes and I, not being on duty, considered ourselves free to do as we pleased, and we held ourselves somewhat aloof, the better to see what was going on. We would not have given up our posts of observation for a good deal.

The English officers impressed us as very unaffected and gentlemanly, whereas the conduct of the other actors in the comedy struck us as decidedly open to criticism. One typical incident amused us greatly, so full was it of absurdity and self-contradiction. We even used a much stronger word, and it was not out of place.) One of the Afrikander nurses had gracefully settled herself in one of the long folding armchairs these ladies carry about with them. She gazed mournfully at the British troops marching in the distance, and, in feeble tones that breathed bitterness, disappointment, and patriotic aversion to the sight of the enemy's uniform, she plaintively—

"How awful it is to have those horrible men all about us! How it sickens me to live so close to them! How I long to escape! Oh, if only—"

The sentence was never finished. The patriotic nurse, as if moved by some hidden spring, suddenly jumped to her feet with a most gracious bow and smile. General Wavell was standing beside her!

Brandely's Farm is a charming spot, a delightful oasis. The inhabitants have fled, in the belief, no doubt, that the English are burning everything in their path. It is bounded by a wood, and has a lovely garden suggestive of Zola's immortal *Paradou*. It was curious to see the mingling of the nurses' white caps and aprons with the English uniforms amidst this brilliant African verdure, and, when a swarm of grasshoppers fell, like a cloud-burst, amongst us, it was still stranger to see the soldiers of the Queen and the nurses of the Republic brandishing hastily-gathered branches, striking out right and left, jumping, shouting, and laughing.

Having wandered apart from the throng to indulge that desire for solitude which all who can separate themselves from the everyday joys and sorrows of life will understand, I found myself within reach of a beautiful flowering tree with golden, sweet-scented blossoms, such as a large mimosa might bear, but with leaves of the acacia variety. I tried to procure a bouquet of branches, but the wood was hard and the thorns were like daggers. With bleeding hands I was about to give up the attempt when three soldiers, who were lying on the ground, and whom I had not seen, rose, and one of them said—

"I'll help you. Sister."

With a large penknife he cut off the best branches and passed them to his comrades, who stripped them of their thorns. When I had enough, they tied the bouquet with grass, and presented it to me.

As I was thanking them, and was about to turn away, I heard a familiar voice greet me with a cheery "Good afternoon, Sister." It was my head attendant from Jacobsdal. We exchanged a good hearty handshake, such as friends and comrades having shared the same humanitarian labours should give each other. Then he said, with all the respect of a soldier addressing his superior officer—

"I am very glad to see you, Sister."

"And so I am to find you here," I replied. "What a pity I haven't got you and Jenny to help me! You were so good to the wounded."

"Why don't you stay with us, Sister?" he asked.

"I cannot, really," I answered. "Lord Roberts will not have women on the battlefield, and so it is my duty, you will understand, to stay with the Boers, in spite of everything." Wishing to test him, I added, "You understand why, don't you?"

He hesitated a few seconds, looked at me with a regret that made itself visible through his outward reserve, and replied—

"Yes, Sister, you are right."

We left the farm last night, two hours after the army had started. They and we are both going to Bloemfontein, though not by the same road. It is even betting as to who will get there first. After three hours' travelling we reached a strange, wild spot, as different as possible from the green and flowery retreat we have so lately left. We are in a great, an immense plain, bordered on the one hand by a range of dark, low hills, and on the other by the shining waters of a small lake, caressed by the rays of a half-awakened, idly moving, undecided moon. With the change of scenery comes a change in the actors. Moving forms appear on the horizon; whether Boers or English we know not. We await developments, and the distant figures are in no hurry to come to close quarters, evidently fearing that our party may turn out to be one of the enemy's patrols. Suddenly we hear shouts of recognition, and about thirty Boers, with bridles hanging loose, dash up from every part of the plain. They are greedy for news in exchange for their own. They are all very hard on Cronje—too hard, in fact. Here, as elsewhere, *les vaincus ont toujours tort*.

Seeing so many nurses and white aprons, and so many different national types, the Boers began to question us. Finding that three of us were Swedes, they asked—

"Have you come all the way from Sweden?"

"No," was the reply. "We live in Johannesburg, and belong to the Swedish Legion."

"Yes," said the Boers; "they fought well.[1] And you?" they inquired, turning to me.

"I come from Belgium," I replied.

"It's a long way off, isn't it? How long were you on the water?"

"Six weeks," I answered; "forty-two days. I was on the *Hertzog*, and the English kept us prisoners a week off Durban."

"And you have come just to nurse our people?" (*ons volk*).

"Certainly."

"Oh, *Zuster*, that is good of you!" said one; "and thank you very much."

"I thank *you*," I replied, "with all my heart. This is the first kind word I have had from a Boer."

"I know," he replied, "they do not all realize what is done for them. It is a great pity."

"At any rate," I said, "that will not prevent us from doing our duty."

"You did quite right," the Swedish nurses afterwards told me, "to speak to him about the Boers' ingratitude. It is altogether too bad sometimes."

We spent a few hours in Petrusberg, and were received in style.

---

1. This legion did indeed fight splendidly. Every man in it was either killed, wounded, or taken prisoner. The Swedish ambulance was then broken up, after Cronje's surrender.

We began with the regulation visit that travelling nurses always pay to their colleagues of the local ambulance. I was surprised to find the German Sisters with whom I came out in the *Hertzog*. After this visit all four of us were seized with a wild desire for new bread, fresh milk, and fresh eggs. The Swedish girls undertook to get the tea ready while I started out to forage. Off I went on my rounds like little Red Riding Hood. I began with the hotel at which I had stopped on my way from Bloemfontein to Jacobsdal.

"Can I have some bread, please?" I asked.

The man to whom I addressed this harmless question flew into such a passion that I thought he was going to strike me.

"I haven't got any bread!" he shouted. "And if I had, do you suppose you would get any?"

"Why not I as well as anyone else? I can pay for it."

"Pay, be hanged!" he yelled. "What about my customers? Where do they come in?"

Poor little Red Riding Hood's round was certainly not beginning too well; but, not being easily discouraged, I continued my walk, peering inquisitively in all directions, and trying to read in people's faces the sort of reception they were likely to give me. Looking through an open door I saw three women in mourning—a thin, sad-eyed, elderly woman and three girls with lovely black eyes, who gazed at me with friendliness in their dark orbs.[2]

"If you please, ladies," I asked, "could you sell me a little new bread?"

They explained that their farm was a long way off, and that the place in which I had found them was merely a sort of *pied-à-terre* to which they never brought more than enough food for the day. The girls, however, whispered among themselves, and one of them spoke to their mother, who said—

"We have still a bottle of fresh milk left. Would you like to have it?"

"Oh, how fortunate!" I exclaimed. "But I hope I shall not be depriving you of it?"

"Oh, *Zuster!*" they all exclaimed with one accord, so spontaneously and with such evident sincerity, so clearly indicating that it would

2. It would be difficult to lay too much stress on the great superiority of the Boer women to the men, I have met some who were endowed with the moat exquisite tact and extraordinary energy, I refer only to the simple and primitive among the Boer women, The half-educated ones are impossible.

have been a pleasure to them to deprive themselves for me, that I accepted the offered milk with heartfelt thanks, not venturing to offer money for it.

"God be with you," said the woman, softly, as I left them. She had lost her husband and one son in the war.

"And may He give you courage," I replied, seeing tears in their tender eyes.

In a store I discovered some fresh eggs which the dealer was kind enough to let me have for a shilling a dozen. This was almost making me a present of them, the market value reaching as much as three shillings. But still there was no sign of bread, and bread I must have, I had already been prowling about for nearly an hour, and what would my comrades think if I came back without it? Just as I was beginning to despair, a delicious odour of freshly baked golden crust, done to a turn, attracted my attention.

"*A la guerre comme à la guerre*" said I to myself; "in you go."

I walked along a passage, and found myself in a small, dark room, which was, nevertheless, light enough to reveal its own unspeakable filthiness. Two women and three men were seated at a table. On it were some of the most appetizing loaves in the world.

"Will you sell me two loaves?" I asked.

If I had called these people thieves and murderers they could not have looked at me more fiercely and angrily than they did.

One of the men rose and shouted—

"Have you got any money? How much will you pay?"

"Whatever you ask," I replied.

"Well, it's"—here he looked at the others as if consulting them—"it's a shilling a loaf."

His companions nodded assent. It was an outrageous price, the loaves being very small, but in spite of the scantiness of my funds, I felt I must have them. I had promised to get bread, and I meant to keep my promise.

"Give me two," I said.

The man took two loaves, but did not offer them to me until he saw me extend my hand to pay him. I tendered him a half-crown, and as he was about to get me the change, I declined it with a gesture, and walked out, my repulsion giving way to amusement at the sight of their sudden satisfaction and respect for the *Zuster* they had treated as a beggar and who was so rich(!).

Rich? Alas! and again alas! I had exactly ten shillings left, and I

58

was not at all sure of finding immediate employment on reaching Bloemfontein. Would the Orange Free State Government give me food and shelter in the meantime? I gave up bothering about the problem, and abandoned myself to the delight I felt in the society of my Swedish friends, who had been so good to me from the first, and so ready to share with me, though I brought nothing into the partnership save gratitude and good humour. What a band of anarchists we were! Among us there were neither chiefs nor subordinates, and no distinctions of social rank, age, or sex; nothing except a fraternal bond of esteem and friendship that united all six of us, and made life bright and happy for us, in spite of the fatigue of our journey.

I need not attempt to describe the joyful cries and wild cheers that greeted me when I arrived with my packages in my apron and the bottle of milk under my arm. The tea was already made, and the sugar and jam were on the festive board. The eggs were soon boiled, and we began to eat in silent enjoyment. We were too intent on our food to talk. We could only exchange looks that expressed the joy of our grateful stomachs. Everything vanished—eggs, bread, and milk—and after the last mouthful, we exclaimed in chorus, replete, happy, and somewhat animalized—"Wasn't that good?"

We have now made two halts since leaving Petrusberg. There is a hot, suffocating wind with nothing whatever to recommend it. The dust gets into our eyes and nose, and covers the food, for which we console ourselves by telling one another that it will clean our teeth beautifully. But it must not be supposed that we were dirty people. Far from it; whenever we met with a rivulet, a lake, or a pond, as we did nearly every day, off we all went in detachments, the men one way and the women the other, to ask the water for a little coolness as well as cleanliness. It was a sight to behold the Afrikander nurses gingerly stepping down to the water on their high heels, with their hair rolled up in a bunch, and to see them again after luncheon, frizzed and curled like so many French poodles, and laced with such appalling tightness that one wondered how they managed to breathe. They wore this panoply even when they were on duty, the Swedish nurses told me. Poor patients!

A despatch rider on the way from Petrusberg to Bloemfontein tells us that the former place has surrendered without striking a blow, and that the English are already at the place where we halted this morning. We should like to move on a little faster, but our unfortunate animals are beginning to suffer severely from the excessive heat and fatigue, and we ourselves are tired out. We have now been bumped and jolted about for nearly a week, and find it ten times more exhausting than the hardest hospital work. Nevertheless, we are as merry as ever, and our amusement increases when we look at each other and notice how very unattractive we are. One of us has caught cold during the night, and is now doubled up with rheumatism in the loins, so that she is obliged to go about all bowed and bent like a centenarian. We are very sorry for her, but it is impossible to preserve our gravity when we see her tottering along, leaning on a stick. She laughs, too, poor thing!

On we go. The Boers encountered *en route* and questioned express a variety of different opinions, some saying there will be a fight to a finish at Bloemfontein, and others that the city will surrender as a matter of course.[3] They all seem to believe, however, that the Transvaal will not prove as accommodating in the matter of surrenders as the Orange Free State, which is considerably Anglicized, and has joined in the fray more in a spirit of kinship with the Boers than through its own convictions. The duration of the war remains very difficult to foretell. When at Jacobsdal I had bet an English officer that it would be all over at the beginning of May, but he and his brother officers felt sure it would last until September at least. I hope I shall prove right, not for the sake of my bet, but for all the lives that will be saved if the fighting ends soon. Quite enough blood has been spilt already on both sides.

---

3. It is worthy of note that the towns which the Boers declared impregnable, and which they would never surrender, gave the English the least trouble of all. Bloemfontein, Kroonstadt, Johannesburg, and Pretoria are instances of this.

CHAPTER 8

Bloemfontein

Here we are at last (on the eve of the British occupation). What am I to do—stay here, or go on to Pretoria by the special train ordered for the ambulance by the Government, the authorities here being always most accommodating for their own people? I put the question to Dr. Dyer, who replied—

"I cannot say, Sister. You are free to do as you please."

This reply was strange, and the doctor's manner was constrained. At Jacobsdal he had been just towards me, and had even advised me to accept the English doctor's offer. Something had no doubt been done on the way to prejudice him against me.

"I beg your pardon, doctor," I said, "but it seems to me you ought to give advice to a Sister who has placed herself under the protection of your ambulance."

He was accustomed to see me always gay, and the firmness of my tone surprised him.

"Come with us to Pretoria," he said.

There being a few hours to spare, I went to see the chief medical officer in the Orange Free State service, and asked if he could make use of me.

"Start as soon as you can," he said. "The English will be here to-morrow."

"That is all the more reason to stay," I rejoined, "as there will be wounded to look after."

"No," he replied; "there will be no fighting."

"What! Is it all over?" I exclaimed.

He shrugged his shoulders, and answered—

"The Government is leaving tonight, and so am I." Abruptly putting out his hand, he added, "Go; and many thanks for all you have

61

done. Sister."[1]

I rejoined my comrades at the railway station, all of us happy at the prospect of spending another day together. We dreaded our approaching separation, knowing that in all probability we should never meet again. There was nevertheless a hope that we might all be put into the same ambulance, but without the Afrikander girls, whose assistance none of us could have accepted.

As we four were standing in a group near the station, I with my back turned to the others, I heard a masculine voice ask them the way. The language used was English, and though the phrases were correct, the voice had an unmistakable accent.

"Oh," I exclaimed, "you must be a Frenchman, *monsieur*."

Society proprieties are not current here, and I could not resist the pleasure of speaking French. I had not heard its dear, familiar sound for so long.

The man whom I thus addressed was equally delighted.

"At last," he exclaimed, "I have found someone who can understand me!"

Then we talked of one thing and another—the war, of course, the Boers, the country, and the climate. This Frenchman in Boer uniform had a frank and open countenance, denoting goodness and intelligence. His manner was marked by the highest distinction, and he impressed me at once as being no ordinary man. Evidently guessing my thoughts, he stopped short, and said—

"I see I must introduce myself. I am Colonel de Villebois, of the French staff."

I returned his confidence by telling him I was from Brussels—a nurse and journalist, but, I believe, omitted to tell him my name. I hope I did abstain, for it was too insignificant to utter in the same breath as that of this brilliant soldier, who had placed his intelligence and devotion at the service of a disappointing people. When he realized that I had left Europe with a purpose similar to his own, a bond of mutual sympathy was established between us at once, and in barely a quarter of an hour from our chance meeting, we were almost as intimate as if we were old friends. He told me, in accents of grief and indignation, of his early enthusiasm and faith in the Boers' courage—a faith that very soon gave way.

"They are only fit for potting game," he said. "They hide behind stones. They are a lot of——"

1. This doctor, for whom I have nothing but praise, was of English origin.

I cannot venture to record the word, although I am beginning to be very much of his way of thinking.

"It is impossible to lead them on!" he exclaimed. "When they have no shelter they run away. If you could only understand the feelings of a soldier when he sees the finest possible positions abandoned! I told Cronje over and over again what was coming, and implored him to act, but he would not listen to anything." [2]

"He is proud and stubborn," I replied, "like all the Boers, but his countrymen are very bitter against him. I am told they consider him responsible for the capture of Jacobsdal, the advance of the English, and the fall of Bloemfontein tomorrow."

"Yes, and without a blow! What a war, and what a people! My eyes are opened now."

"Alas!" I sighed.

"You must have experienced the same feeling of disappointment," he continued, "and suffered accordingly. In the articles you have sent home, have you confessed this disillusionizing you have undergone?"

"No," I replied; "but as my letters have none of their former enthusiasm, I suppose people will read between the lines."

"Yes," he said thoughtfully.

I felt that this man was suffering keenly, and was passing through one of those periods of moral torture in which the greatest and strongest minds experience a weakening of their faith, and feel that they must confide their sorrows in some one. I gave him the kindest and most sympathetic look at my command.

"I dare not tell these things when I write home," he continued; and then he added abruptly, "What would people say if we went back? We should be laughed at, and treated as fools and dupes."

"What does it matter what a lot of idiots say?" I replied. "There is no reason to blush for having been deceived by generous and chivalric ideas. I don't care a straw what they say, and you are beyond the reach of any attack."

And, feeling that he was still depressed in mind, though his expression was cheerful, I changed the subject by asking him what he intended to do next.

"Attack the English in rear, if it is not too late already," he answered. "And where are you going, may I ask?"

---

2. I heard afterwards at Pretoria that Cronje's reply to Colonel de Villebois' remonstranoce was, "Do you think you can teach me to make war? I was fighting before you were born." It is is so idiotic that it must be true.

"To Pretoria, first of all. We all have to go there to await orders when we have finished our work elsewhere."

"If I need any nursing, may you be there to do it!"

Not wishing to let him see how much these simple words had moved me, I laughed, and replied that I hoped he would never need the care of any of us nurses. A gentleman, whom the colonel introduced as his *aide-de-camp*, came up, and, after standing together a few moments longer, we parted. As we shook hands, I thought, "I do hope he will not go and get himself killed." Had not a third person been present, I should have given utterance to the dread that had already begun to haunt me.

After leaving them, I went to fetch my luggage from the hotel, at which I had left it in the belief that I should find employment at Bloemfontein. On my way to the station a second time, I saw the French officers again, and the colonel and I cordially saluted each other.[3]

Our special train to Pretoria did not leave till ten o'clock, four hours after the appointed time. Shortly before we started I happened to meet with one of the young French officers who had come with Colonel de Villebois. Among other remarks he said—

"I have come here chiefly because this is an anti-Semitic war."

"And because you don't like the English, I suppose?"

"No, indeed; it's because I hate the Jews."

"I beg your pardon," I replied, "but I don't quite understand."

"Why," he said, "the Jews are trying to seize the Transvaal gold mines."

"Well, well, you astonish me," I replied. "I thought the person chiefly responsible for the war was Chamberlain, who is a Protestant, and I don't quite see what the Jews have to do with it."

"A great deal, I assure you," he rejoined.[4]

As he was evidently a gentleman, and I could discuss the question with him without fear of being abused, I plunged into the heart of the matter.

"Let me tell you," I said, "that the Jew capitalist is no worse than the Protestant or Catholic. If you cut off this one tentacle, it will grow again, and you will be no better off. You must knock the beast itself on

3. I never saw Colonel de Villebois again. He was killed about a month afterwards.
4. Here is a specimen story I heard on the steamer that brought me back to Europe: The war was the work of the Rothschilds. The Prince of Wales owed them a certain number of millions, and they said, "If we don't have the Transvaal, we will make you a bankrupt," which compelled the Prince to say to Chamberlain, "If you don't declare war, you will be turned out" Gracious! What very determined people!

the head you must kill capitalism. Oh, if people could only be made to understand—"

Here the train started, and I had only just time to jump on it with a hasty goodbye to my anti-Semitic officer. He was in luck's way to escape the lecture with propositions, demonstrations, and conclusions, all complete, that I was about to inflict on him. He would have succumbed under it, without the least doubt.

The first thing to do was to eat the supper my companions had provided. The Government having omitted to light the carriages—it had confined itself to making a contract with the moon, who did her best to carry it out—we fell back on candles. The compartment, which was very comfortable, being provided with a small table, we stuck the candles on the table with some of the melted tallow, and began to eat. It was great fun, especially when a violent jolt threw the candles on to the food and the whole tableful on to our laps. It did us good to laugh so heartily after all the troubles we had gone through, and with others, no doubt, in store for us, but we relapsed into sadness from time to time at the thought that we should soon have to part. The Swedish girls would still be together, but I should have to go on my way alone, and they were sorry for me. I refused to talk about the future, not wishing to depress these dear girls who had been so good to me.

At length we reached Pretoria, they going to a hotel to pass the night before proceeding to their hotel at Johannesburg, and I to join my compatriots, M. and Madame ———, who treated me with the utmost kindness and hospitality. I said goodbye to my dear companions next day at the railway station, in the hope that I should obtain charge of an ambulance and have them with me.[5]

---

5. To my great regret, we never met again.

CHAPTER 9

Pretoria

This little town is really very pretty. In ordinary times it must be a restful sort of place. Except for two business streets of handsome and well-stocked shops, the town consists of single- storied villas, buried in flowers and verdure. Pretoria and Johannesburg form a complete contrast. Before the war, Johannesburg was a lively, bustling, cosmopolitan city, but now it is dull and desolate, all its animation having been transferred to Pretoria. Officers, soldiers, doctors, nurses, and attendants, all have to come here for orders. There are incessant comings and goings, the hotels are crammed, the cab-horses have no rest, and the station is one perpetual block of wounded coming, troops going, people hanging about for want of something better to do, and relatives and friends greeting or bidding farewell to those dear to them. There are scenes of mute but acute despair, and there are also, unknown to those who do not look for them, incidents of the most grotesque and ridiculous kind—displays of vanity such as I cannot describe here.[1]

The negro dandies one sees on Sundays are highly amusing. They are simply running over with style. Their get-up consists of a smoking- jacket, white trousers worn very long, white shoes, a stiff collar coming up to the ears and encircling the neck like a *garotte*, a light-coloured tie, a white straw hat balanced on the forehead and the tip of the nose, a stick in the hand, and a flower in the buttonhole. In this guise they sally forth to fascinate their negresses, who wear light dresses with trains, and walk along with measured step, the bust thrown well forward, the hips prominent, and the waist laced and corseted to

---

1. This sort of thing attained tremendous proportions later on. I spent some time with two foreign field-officers in the Transvaal service, who each told me what a pity it was he could not make something of the other! I could never find out which had the higher rank in the Boer service, and I imagine each of them was firmly convinced that he was the superior.

incredible slimness.

What clod-hoppers the Boers seem in comparison with this clever, intelligent, and active race! To think that most of the cabbies—little nigger boys of twelve or fourteen—speak English, Dutch—and nigger, of course! I just love them! These blacks are amusing, kind-hearted, original, and very intelligent. The Boers have swindled and robbed them, and driven them out and maltreated them. If I were a Kaffir, shouldn't I chuckle now! There is a day of reckoning for nations as well as for individuals. *All they that take the sword shall perish with the sword*, is eternally true.

I have made the acquaintance of a French officer, Lieutenant Galopaud, who is in command of a detachment of French volunteers. He is an elegant cavalier of adventurous character and, perhaps, rather devil-may-care disposition, but the most obliging of men. He also has got over his enthusiasm for the Boers.

"Do you know," he said, "I have had enough of risking my life for these fellows. I am ready to fight and do my duty, but when it comes to getting a bullet through you while they are running away, I draw the line at that."

I told him he was quite right.

Being very anxious to go to the front, I paid a visit to the State Secretary, Mr. Reitz, and his wife—a beautiful and deservedly esteemed Dutchwoman, who was very kind to the foreign nurses—to ask for a letter of introduction to the Medical Committee. I handed this letter, which was couched in the most flattering terms, to the Secretary of the Committee, who read it, and asked me very angrily why I had asked for it.

"So that you should know what I have done and what I want," I replied, "seeing that you don't know me."

"We know quite well who you are and what you have done," he said. "This letter is of no use at all."

"Still, I should have thought the State Secretary—"

"He has nothing to do with it."

"Very good," I said, inwardly observing that this must be a queer country for a subordinate official to talk about the State Secretary in this style. "Will you send me to the front?"

"Certainly, Sister," he replied, mollified. "You fully deserve it."

That word "deserve" was rich! Apparently professional nurses who know their business thoroughly are expected to give proofs of courage and capability before they are granted the honour of going to the front, and this for no other reason than that they are foreigners, the Boers having a deep-rooted scorn and dislike for anything appertaining to countries not their own.

On the other hand, Boer women, without the slightest notion of nursing the sick or bandaging wounds, are entrusted with the most important posts. Doctors who had to put up with such helpers have had a good deal to say about them.

"But," continued the secretary, "I do not think there is any opening for you at present. You will have to wait a little."

Here a messenger entered with a telegram.

"You are in luck," exclaimed the secretary, after reading it. "Here is a wire asking for a doctor and chief nurse for Mafeking. Will you go?"

"There is no fighting at Mafeking," I said.

"But there will be. I tell you so in confidence. Are you willing."

"I suppose so," I said, without much enthusiasm.

"Very well, then. Get ready, ask for your railway pass and your passport, and tomorrow morning you will he told at what time you have to start. You are not to wait for any one. The doctor will not come for forty-eight hours."

"I shall be ready," I replied; and left him, far from satisfied and vaguely suspecting that he was deceiving me. I soon met with a foreign doctor and confided my doubts to him.

"Mafeking?" he exclaimed. "Don't go; you will have nothing but typhoid cases."

"I hear there's to be some fighting."

"Humbug!" he said. "Innocent person, do you still believe what a Boer says?"

"Hardly," I replied.

"Very well, then," he continued. "Take my advice, and refuse to go. You have already had more than your share of typhoids."

"I should just think I have; but I can't refuse now, after having promised."

"Promised?" he repeated. "You are really extraordinary. Don't you see the man has been telling you lies?"

"Are you quite sure?" I asked.

"You'll soon see."

"Anyhow," I said, "I am booked, and there's an end of it. I must go."

"Very well, then," he retorted. "Go; and I hope you will enjoy yourself." [2]

Next morning, not having received my promised marching orders, I set out for the Medical Committee's office, and met Lieutenant Galopaud and a French nurse, Madame Thouvenot, for whom her obliging countryman was trying to find employment. Galopaud had friends at court, and it did not take him long to obtain a promise that we should both be sent to the front, either at Christiana or Fourteen Streams, "the most dangerous place of all," we were told. As we were both ready for anything, we willingly undertook to go, especially as the Boer ambulance doctors would not allow their Sisters to risk their lives too rashly. We started next day. Lieutenant Galopaud, who was about to join Colonel de Villebois, promised to organize an ambulance, appoint us to it, and attach it to the Foreign Legion, under the colonel's command. The fulfilment of his complimentary desire to be under my care in case of need would thus come within the range of possibility.

---

2. He was quite, right The Boer had told me an abominable lie. There was not the least prospect of fighting at Mafeking about this time.

CHAPTER 10

On the Jaunt

Klerksdorp, March 20.—We are waiting here until the Boers shake off enough of their slowness and indifference to supply us with a vehicle, animals, and driver. This morning we were told to wait two days more and go by the mail! This was not exactly in harmony with my instructions from the Transvaal Minister of Posts and Telegraphs, whom I had met at Pretoria and Jacobsdal. Seeing me at a station while he was passing through, he shouted—"Look sharp, *Zuster*, you'll be wanted."

At last! We are to go to Christiana by the mail-cart leaving here at two o'clock tomorrow morning, and arriving there on the morning of the next day. We are to stay at Christiana until further notice.

Christiana March 27.—This Red Cross organization and the orders from the Medical Committee are a marvel of muddle and carelessness! Madame Thouvenot, who has only just arrived in Africa, and has not yet lost her illusions, now sees the real state of affairs displaying itself in its far from attractive nakedness. She complains, and I tell her she is only at the beginning of her troubles. We are supposed to be at the front, but there is just as little fighting hero as at Mafeking, We have now been twiddling our thumbs for a week. Failing to understand why we were sent to this place, we went to the hospital, and interviewed the head surgeon, Dr. Dunlop, an Englishman living here, whose skill saved the life of the Creusot engineer (I have forgotten his name). He told us that he telegraphed to Pretoria for a second nurse. Pretoria wired back, "Sending two first nurses," to which he replied, "Cannot employ them." That did not make any difference to the gentlemen in Pretoria, and they packed us off without more to-do. It was too funny, and I laughed heartily.

"You seem to find everything amusing," my companion said

gloomily.

"Why," I replied, "if I had wept over every scurvy trick that has been played me since I came to this country I should have no eyes left, and there would be nothing for it but to ask the Boer Government for a little dog and a clarionet."

As there was no work for us at the hospital, I wired to Pretoria for permission to return. Forty-eight hours later came an order to stay. I telegraphed again; no answer.

We are staying at the hotel, kept by some Germans, who are very nice and obliging people. Many Boers drop in for a glass or more—generally more. A few Boers—the big guns these—dine here sometimes. They are very lively. They dance, sing, and play hymns and polkas on the organ. We hold aloof from them. My companion does not understand either English or Dutch, and I feel an unconquerable repugnance to associate with men who can be so gay while their country is fighting for its existence. Men are just as vain as women, and the young sparks do their best to attract our attention by their jokes and sallies of wit. One of them, thinking to distance all the others, took the hotel cat, a very pretty and gentle creature, and stuck his lighted cigarette into its mouth. The poor cat howled with pain, to the intense amusement of the festive gathering. Feeling that it was a pity not to respond to such amiable advances, I rose, and, looking the fellow full in the face, said—

"*Verken!*" (hog).

They laughed again, but were not at their ease, and soon left the room. They must have come to the conclusion that I did not understand their kind of wit, and that points of contact between us were wanting.

The Dutch whom I had told of the treatment we received from the Pretoria Committee were indignant, and mentioned the matter to some of the Boer officers, with the result that Commandant De Beers paid us a visit. An excellent, big-hearted man, this I He folded us poor distressed nurses to his broad chest, after which he complained of pains in the region of the heart, and wanted to be examined.

"By-and-by, commandant," I said. "You are too nervous just now."

He came again later on, with some difficulty. He was less nervous this time, and we were able to talk. He listened attentively, said I had acted properly, and summed up by declaring that the Government was doing nothing but blunder. He promised we should have a reply by telegraph or another visit from him within two days; that, in the former case, we should be sent to Fourteen Streams; and that, in the second, he would bring us our tickets for Pretoria. We are now waiting.

In the meantime, I may as well record a serio-comic incident that happened on our way hither. It suggests Paul Louis' "Shall we kill them both?"[1]and might be entitled *The Frightened Landdrost* (a sort of local judge or district commissioner). We had left Klerksdorp at two o'clock in the morning, and about three hours later a wheel collapsed, compelling us to sit, half-frozen, on the ground while our driver went to look for another vehicle, after which we resumed our journey as best we could. Our travelling companions were an Anglo-Boer hospital attendant—who was as charming as all others of this mixed race—and a Dutchman, the *landdrost* above mentioned, with both of whom we fraternized and shared our provisions. While we were stopping to change animals, Madame Thouvenot and I, the heat being very great, climbed into one of the unharnessed vehicles, and very foolishly ensconced ourselves at the back. Suddenly Madame Thouvenot exclaimed—

"Oh, look!"

"What's the matter?"I asked.

"The pole!"

There was no doubt about it. The pole was rising, at first slowly, and then suddenly, until it pointed heavenwards. We poor things were hurled to the end of the cart as it tilted over with a crash. We were simply buried under baggage of all kinds, with our knees jammed against our noses, and our heads enveloped in the folds of our capes. Our position must have been the most elegant imaginable, and would have delighted the heart of a photographer. For a few seconds everyone was paralyzed, The men, thinking us squeezed to a jelly, stood motionless with horror. As for us, we expected another avalanche of baggage to follow, and flatten us out completely. Then we broke out into loud laughter, to the great relief of our companions. Only the *landdrost*, who was seized with convulsive tremors, failed to join in the general hilarity.

On arriving here, I was attacked with increasingly severe pains, and

---

1. An allusion to Paul Louis Courier's story of the two frightened travellers who, having taken shelter for the night in a woodcutter's hut, heard their host put the above-quoted question to his wife, and imagined that their last hour had come, whereas the remark applied to the chickens intended for the travellers' meal.— Translator.

a large abscess formed on my hip. The doctor told me the accident had had more effect on me than on my companion, my blood having been thinned by privations, bad food and want of nourishment, to say nothing of having been poisoned at Jacobsdal.

In looking through my notes I see I have not mentioned this last incident. I will now repair the omission, for what reason will be seen later on.

After the Boers had refused me food, and before I had obtained it through General Wavell's intercession, I remained hungry for several days. Of course I did not accept my English patients' sweet offer to share their rations, but I was very glad of a tin of corned beef, which I owed to the generosity of my head attendant. He warned me that it would not be fit to eat after the second day. I dined off it that day, the next, and again the third day. It smelt so good, and I was so hungry that I could not resist it. My imprudence brought speedy punishment. I was almost immediately seized with violent pains, syncope, and fever that remained three hours at the very respectable temperature of 104°. I took a glass of brandy—some was still left, fortunately—and lay down, fully dressed, asking myself whether I should be able to resume my duties in the evening or have to say goodbye to the innumerable joys of life. It was a serious problem, and I sank into a heavy slumber before I had solved it. I woke just in time to receive a fresh batch of wounded.

"I came your way this afternoon, Sister," said my head attendant, "and saw you were lying down. Weren't you all right?"

"Oh, my good fellow," I replied, "I was frightfully ill"; and I related what had occurred.

"But I had some more corned beef, and I could have given you some that was fresh," he exclaimed.

"I should not have taken it," I replied. "It must be saved for the wounded."

"The Sister comes first," he said indignantly.

"Thanks with all my heart," I rejoined, "but I put the wounded first."

After this digression I return to my abscess and the *landdrost*.

For several days I endured maddening pain. It was decided that I must be lanced—and pretty deeply, I knew. Dr. Dunlop, who was very busy, could only come at night, between one and two o'clock, while everyone else in the hotel was asleep. He forgot to bring an anaesthetic, and offered to go back for it; but I could stand the pain no longer, and preferred to have the operation over.

"It will hurt you," he said. "Take your handkerchief, and bite hard on it when I begin."

I promised to be brave, but, when I felt the lancet apparently cutting right through my body, I gave way, and shrieked like a walloped donkey or a member of Parliament called to order. The honest *land-drost*, who was sleeping in the next room, woke with a start, jumped out of bed, threw on a few garments, and rushed out with his revolver, in the belief that some Kaffirs had got into our room. He hurled himself against the garden door, but found it bolted. Then he ran to our window, which was on the ground floor, and saw that it was open, with the blind down and a light inside. Hearing groans, and still full of the idea that the Kaffirs were trying to murder us, he was about to push the blind aside and climb into the room when he heard the voices of Dr. Dunlop and Madame Thouvenot. Then, knowing I was ill, he guessed what was going on, and went back to bed.

"I couldn't sleep a wink all the rest of the night," the good man told me when he paid me a visit nest day. He was still too upset to laugh at the incident.

Here I must take the opportunity of expressing my gratitude to Dr. Dunlop for his great kindness to me. He came to see me three times a day, and was so afraid I should develop fever that I had to reassure him. He also brought me wine to give me a fillip. (A nurse travelling at the expense of the Transvaal Government is entitled to nothing in the shape of liquids except water and tea. She is better treated in the Orange Free State; while I was at Bloemfontein I was allowed a glass of beer with my meals.) In short, he was a true doctor—that is to say, his patient's friend—and I cannot express the gratitude I feel towards him.

It has now been decided that Madame Thouvenot and I are to start shortly for Fourteen Streams with a young doctor belonging to the Russian ambulance, who has recently arrived here. Fighting is expected at Fourteen Streams, and Commandant De Beers tells me that the biggest battle since the beginning of the war may take place there. As complaints have been made that the stations for giving first aid to the wounded are too far from the battlefield, we are to install ourselves at the railwaystation, about four thousand yards from the zone of fire, and stay there as long as the place is tenable.

The Russian doctor did not at first appear altogether delighted at the prospect of having us for helpers. This was understandable, as all the ambulances—except the Belgian, which was broken up on reaching Pretoria—work together. Moreover, this Russian ambulance, the second, was landed six weeks ago, but has not yet found anything to do, and the doctor to whom we are to be tacked on was sent here merely as a sort of advance guard. We insist on our rights, officially certified from Pretoria, and, moreover, we are wanted at the front. The Boer combatants, on being consulted (!), approved of us as nurses, and finally a telegram from General Potgieter, stating that we should be of the greatest use, and that we were to start with the Russian doctor, put an end to the conflict, which was a courteous one throughout.[2]

March 29.—Another telegram from the general, telling us to start to-morrow. I am not good for much, and am threatened with a second abscess, unfortunately. However, we can lay a mattress in the ambulance waggon, which will thus be put to its proper use. We are to "hurry up," it seems. More bloodshed, more suffering, more deaths! Poor fellows!

The promised ambulance waggon has not come; we are taking an ancient landau instead. The eight hours' travelling will be trying for me. That is a detail, but are the sick and wounded to be carted about in this wretched conveyance? No ambulance waggon, and not a drop of brandy or champagne for the poor exhausted creatures we shall have to try to revive! Oh, what a state of things one has to put up with here! To think that the *Dames de France* have sent enormous quantities of alcohol of different kinds, that the cases were at Pretoria, that the French nurse who is with me could get none of it, and that the French Sisters' admirable charity has so little benefited the unfortunate men to whom their pitying hearts went out!

---

2. I still have this telegram from General Potgieter. He was acting for General Du Toit, who was unwell. It is rather valuable, departing as it does from the accepted order of things, and giving direct instructions to nurses over the doctor's head.

CHAPTER 11

Fourteen Streams

April 6.—We arrived here on Sunday—Dr. Weber, surgeon of the Mary Magdalene Hospital, St. Petersburg, Madame Thouvenot, and myself. The "locality" consists of exactly five buildings—the station, the hotel and refreshment-room, the post and telegraph office, a warehouse, the station-master's residence, and nothing else; not even a hut. On the other side of the river is a small village, Warrenton, where the English are encamped. We have established ourselves in the station-master's house. It has been completely stripped; even the locks have vanished. If the English had been here, these robberies would have been put down to their account; but, as it is, they cannot be accused. Our accommodation is extraordinary! Some empty provision cases serve as chairs, and we have broken up others and made them into tables. Stretchers are our beds. There is hardly anything to eat, and for twenty-four hours we have had nothing to drink; not even a drop of the brackish water that is sowing the seeds of typhus in the neighbouring laagers.

General Du Toit came to see us the other day, He is a very good-looking man, as polished as a prison door; quite the opposite of De Beers, who is too expansive, Du Toit says the position is a dangerous one, to which Dr. Weber replies, "The Sisters were told as much at Pretoria, and they will be more useful in this advanced post than elsewhere."

These Russians have a really marvellous knack of picking up languages. Dr. Weber has been less than two months in this country, but, with a little help from German, he understands Flemish as well as I do, and talks *taal* with the utmost ease.

Since Sunday there has been a little artillery firing every morning. Dr. Weber asserts that the object is to keep the Boers quiet while the English are bathing! It is quite likely; there are queer doings here. One thing there can be no doubt about is that the Boers are acting just as they did at Jacobsdal—that is to say, letting the enemy make his preparations,[1] in spite of a telegram received yesterday from Father Kruger asking why the Boers do not attack.

We have no patients, but are far from having no bombardment. This is my second, and I have hitherto escaped without a scratch; but *sapristi*! Madame la Mort has sneezed very near us. It occurred this afternoon. None of the Boers who came for medical attendance this morning anticipated an attack. The smallness of their number was the best proof of this. Whenever there is a prospect of a big fight, they come *en masse* to ask for a medical certificate of illness, so that they can get leave of absence. Madame Thouvenot and I (the doctor being on his rounds at the laager) were quietly sitting in front of our door this afternoon when there was a sudden bang in the distance, followed by a whiz and a crash. It was a shell!

The shock was decidedly unpleasant at first, but we got over it fairly quickly. We instinctively stooped, expecting the house to fall about our ears. As it did nothing of the kind, we looked at each other.

"We are in for it, my dear," observed my companion.

"Right in the thick of it," I responded.

A second shell came, followed by a third, and then a fourth. Nevertheless, we stayed where we were, although we were not called upon to do so, the ambulance being empty. Then we saw a group of men take to flight. They were the railway and telegraph hands, and in the forefront was a Boer combatant, running for dear life.

"Oh, look!" exclaimed Madame Thouveuot, laughing heartily, "there's the captain deserting his ship!"

"What a brave lot they are!" I responded, remembering my Jacobsdal attendants.

"*Gant vlengt, Zusters!*" ("Run, Sisters "), shouted our brave commander,

"What does he say?" asked Madame Thouvenot.

I translated the Boer's *patois*.

"Tell him that's all very well for him," she said.

---

1. Fourteen Streams was not captured until sometime afterwards. It was taken by surprise, although General Du Toit thought himself secure from attack. Sudden turning movements have formed the basis of the English tactics, and the Boers invariably fell headlong into the trap. I refer, of course, to real battles, and not to the present guerrilla warfare.

"I have, confound him!" I replied, enraged and humiliated.

The cowardice of this Fleming made my own Flemish blood boil within me. No outsider had seen the flight at Jacobsdal, but here, before a foreigner, I would have given anything to prevent this.

We next saw a forlorn couple making their way towards us, the husband almost dragging his poor wife, who was half dead with fright. They were English, and the Boers had refused them food because the man would not fight against those of his own blood. The Boers had also declined to let them reach the frontier. During the last few days we had shared our scanty rations with them, sending our blacks with what we could spare to the hotel, where the couple were allowed to stay and look after the building.

They were still a few paces from us when their dwelling flew up into the air like a champagne cork. A good shot, that; right in the bull's eye. It was decidedly curious to see the furniture whirl heavenwards, and fall in clusters like fireworks. Then the railway-station and post-office went; not blown up, but knocked down. Our house was now the only building left. We were right in the line of fire, and were thus infringing the Geneva rules. Moreover, our Red Cross flag was not flying, and the English were fully entitled to fire at us; but they doubtless saw our white caps and aprons through their telescopes, and took care to spare the Sisters, for whom they have such great respect. For the moment, however, we were ignorant of their intentions, and whether they knew who the denizens of the stationmaster's house were. I admit that it was obstinate and idiotic on ray part, but I burned to display our Red Cross flag. Soldiers, who hold to their own colours, will understand our pride in our ensign of pity and mercy.

"Aren't you afraid?" I asked the Englishman, who had handed his wife over to the care of Madame Thouvenot.

"No, Sister," he replied.

"Very good;" and when the next shell had burst, we sallied out and fixed the flag.

Bang, fo-o-o-ot, bang I We rushed out again, but had gone only a few yards when another shell burst quite near us and near Madame Thouvenot, who was watching us from the door.

"We must go, Sister," said the Englishman. "You will get killed, and it is useless to stay here when the ambulance is empty."

He was right; and, there being nothing less like real courage than bravado, we started. The shells were falling like hail, rarefying the air about us. At every bang we threw ourselves full length in the brush-wood. Then we picked ourselves up, crawled a few yards on our hands and knees, and started off again. It was a game of hide-and-seek with Death. After the first few minutes it became quite amusing, and we should have laughed heartily but for the sight of the poor little fainting, almost dying, woman and her distressed husband.

The bombardment lasted a good half-hour. We returned at nightfall, and encountered our chief, who had rushed back in a terrible state, he having been told that the ambulance had been blown up and the Sisters killed. We also encountered a young Boer of eighteen, who belonged to the postal service, and spoke English admirably. He was weeping for joy.

"There you are at last. Sister!" he said. "When we came back after the bombardment, I went to the ambulance at once to see if you were there. I hunted everywhere and called your name time after time, but there was no reply, and I thought you were killed, but here you are. I'm so glad!"

How comforting it was, this hitherto unsuspected affection that had blossomed in the hour of danger! I thanked the dear fellow with all my heart. I do not even know his name, and, most probably, I shall never see him again. The telegraph-station is to be removed a long way from here, and the only human beings near us will depart. As for the English couple, we have offered them our hospitality.

The Boers, under General Du Toit, have at last arrived with their artillery, and tomorrow there will be plenty of noise on both sides. Our flag has now been hoisted, and we hope to be able to stay here. If we have to go, we shall return after the bombardment, and attend to the wounded.

I must here note a fairly typical conversation that has just taken place between General Du Toit and myself. It was after today's bombardment. Night was coming on. The general was inspecting the ruins, and I, still haunted by my one idea, went up to him to ask for two of his men to hoist our flag on our ambulance roof The general pretended not to see me, though my white dress must have been prominent enough. To my request he answered—

"Why?"

"So that the English will not fire on the ambulance and kill our wounded."

He began to laugh, and said, "Do you think the flag will prevent that? They will fire just the same."

"It's not true, general. They won't."

"What do you know about it?" he asked roughly.

"I know they did not fire on my hospital at Jacobsdal when it was full of *van u volk* (your people), and you have no right to say they will do it here," I rejoined.

I was now thoroughly sick of the lies and calumnies and blusterings I had heard for months. It was enough to make one throw up one's immortal soul! As the brave general gave no answer, I turned my back on him and returned to the ambulance. Our blacks, who had returned, managed to hoist the flag with Dr. Weber's help.

7th, Morning.—Sharp firing at daybreak; everything quiet now. Some Boers come, and I ask if there are any wounded.

"None on our side," they reply, "but the English have lost some men."

"How many?"

"Twenty at least."

"Then," I said, "they have only thirty soldiers left, and yet they have a general and a staff."

"But, *Zuster*——"

"That's so," I said. "You told me the day before yesterday there were only fifty English on the other side of the river."

They laughed awkwardly. They had forgotten having said there were only fifty of the enemy, and no doubt congratulated themselves on not having put the number of wounded at sixty instead of twenty.

The effects of the bombardment are very curious. The telegraph office is in a sad state. The batteries are all in a heap, and the wires twisted into a ball. The doors and windows are torn off and smashed to atoms. The hotel is a shapeless mass of bits of furniture, kitchen utensils, bottles, lamps, and various articles reduced to powder. The building itself is a mere heap of planks. Pick up some bits of shell, of course, as at Jacobsdal; am quite a magnet in attractiveness for the English fire. Having ventured amongst the ruins, I hear plaintive sounds, faint at first, but afterwards developing into unmistakable mewing. I call, "Pussy, pussy," and two loves of cats, who have miraculously escaped death, show themselves. I restore these victims of the war to their owners, the English couple staying with us.

Their chickens were less fortunate. Every one of them was killed by lyddite. The fumes turned them quite yellow, so that they looked like some new and strange kind of canary. Madame Thouvenot and I thought ourselves lucky to find something to eat, and we set to work to pluck the unlucky birds, in spite of the coughing caused by the emanations from the terrible explosive with which their feathers were saturated. Unfortunately, we were obliged to abandon our hopes. Our chief did not share our enthusiasm, and made us throw the fowls away.

Tonight the Boers have altered the position of their guns, which are now on the left of our ambulance. The English artillery is on our right. A pleasant position for us! Dr. Weber insists on our all three going away tomorrow, and not returning until nightfall. We object, and finally carry our point. The poor doctor was terribly upset the other day, thinking his nurses were killed, and he is not anxious to go through such a time again.

Sunday Afternoon 8th.—Dr. Weber and Madame Thouvenot having taken advantage of the day of rest to drive to one of the *laagers*, I offered my services to take care of the house, which has no locks, and look after the blacks. Seeing that I am unarmed, and that not a single door will shut, I should have some difficulty in defending the place. Indeed, I might be knocked on the head fifty times without any one being the wiser. Nevertheless, I am not in the least afraid; but suddenly a fit of melancholy seizes me, and I begin to long for my far-away home. This strikes me as silly, and I try to laugh it off, but without success. Then I lecture myself severely, and endeavour to make believe that a nurse's country is where her patients are. Finally, I say to myself, "Write; it will make you forget your physical sufferings, and drive away this shameful depression."

Thereupon, having some hours of leisure before me, I return to my diary, and proceed to record some impressions which the all-absorbing work at Jacobsdal prevented me from noting. At the present moment, however, it is atrociously hot, our boys (black servants) are keeping up an incessant chattering, and the horrible, maddening buzzing of the flies is becoming worse and worse. These creatures make life a misery to us. They torture us all day until about six o'clock in the afternoon; they get into your nose, eyes, and ears, and into your mouth when you drink; and they drop into your food while you eat it. They make me regret the Jacobsdal mice and ants, which were little loves in comparison with this horrible winged carrion.

Jacobsdal! My work there was hard, but fascinating, and far preferable to my present inaction. Here we do nothing but wait for something to happen; and though the three of us get on very well, we have little in common. Dr. Weber is afraid the Russian nurses will not like his being here with foreigners. As for us, we should very much like to be sent to join the Foreign Legion, and we are on the lookout for a telegram from Colonel de Villebois.[2] From time to time, when friction occurs, my fellow-nurse indignantly exclaims—

"What's the good of the Franco-Russian alliance, I should like to know?"

"You see, my dear," I replied, "this interesting case was not foreseen when the alliance was contracted. We shall have to send a note to the two powers."

"Oh, one never knows when to take you seriously," she said, in a huff.

Meanwhile, behold the Franco-Russian alliance going about in a landau, drawn by four horses, and driven by our Indian coachman. It is a spanking turn-out, and no mistake, is it not? But what a pity we have such bad food, and so little of it!

Our black boys are singing. These robbed and defrauded human beings are actually singing! The Boers, after waging a disgraceful war on them, steeping so many of them in blood and taking away their all, treat them as brutes and outlaws. But, for all that, if there be an interesting, intelligent, perfectible race, it is these blacks. As servants they are rather slow, and sometimes lazy, but you can do as you like with them when they feel themselves loved and humanely treated, instead of (as is generally the case) as filthy animals.

My two blacks from Jacobsdal, Piet and John, deserve a short description here. They are very different in looks and character, but are both good, honest fellows, and have served me devotedly. They have done all that was possible in their positions as hospital attendants to help the *Missi*, It was useless to tell them to call me Sister, and remind them that blacks and whites are as much brothers and sisters as blacks are to each other. They never dared to do it, and could only reply, in confusion, "Oh no, *Missi*; oh no, *Missi*." Poor creatures! To think that much of this timidity arises from fear and distrust of the whites, who have so long tyrannized over them!

Piet was overflowing with inexhaustible gaiety, and was a great hand at catching mice. Sometimes these rodents took too great liberties with us, such as steeple-chasing over our noses at night with squeaks of joy, much to our annoyance. On these occasions he used to catch the mice in our room. When asleep, he was insensible to everything. I remember a laughable scene that I witnessed one night at the hospital. Piet was snoring in a corner, and a large, wavy lizard was

2. He was dead before I wrote these lines.

taking his ease with evident enjoyment on the sleeper's neck and face. From time to time, Piet, without waking, made a movement as if to drive away the intruder, who, as soon as he was knocked over, climbed up again, got caught in the woolly hair, freed himself, and tumbled down again towards the neck.

As the snorer opened his mouth wide, and the visitor was rather too near, I woke the good fellow, fearing that the lizard might be engulfed in the abyss. Another night, not having enough boiled water for my patients, I set off in the direction of our kitchen, a sort of vestry of the Kaffir church we were using as a hospital, and called Piet. He did not reply. I opened the outer door and called again, with no result. Then, being struck by the lovely view of the immense surrounding plain, lit up by the moon with a. peculiarly romantic grandeur, not unmixed with sadness, such as I have never noticed elsewhere, I stood lost in admiration of the sight, too beautiful for earth! Then I resumed control of my wandering senses, and became a busy nurse again.

"Piet!" I cried.

No answer.

Fearing that my faithful black had met with some accident, I went out to look for him, but as I began to descend the steps I put my foot on something soft, and, in my efforts to preserve my balance, I took a terrific header into the sand—one of those tumbles that one does not forget in a hurry. I picked myself up quickly, fearing that the body on the steps betokened some tragedy, approached, and beheld my Piet snoring the snores of the just. I divined the drama that had taken place: he had gone to fetch water, and had come back, mounted one step, found that the second was altogether too much for him, lain down and gone to sleep. He certainly had a great deal to do.

"Piet, Piet!"

No reply. I poked him harder.

"Hi, Piet, old boy!"

He opened his eyes, saw me, and was seized with an uncontrollable fit of laughter, interspersed with volleys of "Yes, *Missi*! yes, *Missi*!" but not budging an inch. As I was unable to keep from laughing, and it would not do for me to lose all authority, I went in.

Piet thought I was angry, and followed me. Angry with him, poor fellow!

In another scene I remember my professional decorum completely forsook me, and at a time, too, when laughter might be considered cruel by the tender souls and good people whom any departure from the ordinary run of daily life upsets and disturbs. But really, if a nurse on active service were to give way to sickly sentimentalism, her position would be untenable. Our hospital accommodation was very poor, and the shrouding of the dead had to be done behind a screen in the ward containing twenty-two Boer typhoid patients. The business was still more complicated at night The heat was so frightful that the candles either doubled up or melted and fell on the bed or the operator.

A gust of wind, too, would occasionally blow the door open and extinguish the lights. The incident in question happened on one of these stormy nights. I was shrouding a corpse—the second within a few hours. The *sirocco* whistled and howled outside, and waves of sand dashed themselves against the windows until we could easily, but for the absence of motion, have imagined ourselves at sea. The door, in spite of the big stones we had piled against it, suddenly flew open. The screen was knocked over, the candle also, and, in the dim light of early morning, the dead man was revealed. He was, I remember, a fine big fellow of thirty-eight, who was brought here in a delirious, hopeless state after twenty days' illness at the *laager*, and who always said "Thank you, father" ("*Dank ce, fader*") when I gave him anything to drink. His dying agonies had convulsed his features, and his expression in death was ghastly.

Close to him were two patients, one of whom was delirious and the other slightly mad. They caught sight of the awful face, and there was a terrible to-do. The lunatic jumped out of his bed and took refuge in that of his delirious comrade, who, still more frightened, yelled and struggled desperately in vain attempts to break loose. I tried to separate them, but they were big, strong men, and I had to abandon the attempt. I replaced the screen and relit the candle, whereupon the rest of the patients, seeing what was going on, began to laugh like so many schoolboys. In an unfortunate moment I called Piet. The sight threw him into convulsions of mirth, and he rolled on the floor, absolutely helpless. The couple on the bed were bobbing up and down in intensely comical attitudes, their arms and legs whirling round like the sails of a windmill, and Piet's collapse increased the patients' laughter to a perfect paroxysm. I ought to have scolded Piet, but was scarcely in a condition to do it, for I was literally choking. After this I was convinced that dying of laughter is an impossibility.

Such was Piet, the embodiment of gaiety and loquacity. John, on the other hand, was the personification of silence. He sometimes smiled, but never laughed. His expression was reflective, his eyes were full of meaning, and he was a much more efficient helper than Piet. When there were three of us nurses, Piet liked us all, but John displayed a marked preference for me. His respect was almost religious. When on night duty he never slept, but responded to my lightest word, and always spared me the heavy work. When I gave an order, he bowed. When he brought me anything he seemed as if something prompted him to kneel. I often caught him gazing at me in a sort of adoration, mingled with exalted devotion and some curiosity. He was a big strong fellow, and could have broken me in two like a reed, but he was always hovering about me as if I were a child whom it was his duty to protect.

I often wondered what thoughts were passing through this undeveloped brain. Did he regard me as a being of a superior order or a priestess of kindness because I spoke to him as no one had ever done? I suppose so, but I never questioned him or sought to discover the springs of his mind, so primitive, so beautifully receptive to those feelings of which we civilized beings are gradually losing all knowledge. In him gratitude and devotion could reach their utmost limits.

How very few of these Boers possess even the instinctive gratitude an animal feels when helped or relieved, and how great is the contrast between the Boers and these blacks! The latter are infinitely superior. The Kaffirs, I am convinced, could be made an exceptionally fine race, full of life and originality, and eager for intellectual and moral development.[3] Here the black is regarded as something lower than a pig is considered by us. His church is always relegated to a considerable distance from the town or village, as if he and his fellows were plague-stricken. In certain hospitals they are still huddled apart in some out-of-the-way corner, and in such institutions as treat them comparatively well the fact is always carefully brought into prominence.

A Boer would think himself dishonoured or polluted if he and a black slept in the same room. This reminds me that when my fellow-nurse, who was of English parentage, was suffering from typhus at

3. One of the passengers on board the *Messageries Maritimes* steamer which brought me back to Europe was a young Swiss Protestant missionary who had spent nearly two years in educating and refining the Transvaal blacks. He had an enthusiastic admiration for them, and was always extolling their good qualities. He was never weary of dwelling upon their love of study, their capacity for learning, and their boundless desire for knowledge. "Educate these people," he said, "and in only three generations the results will be marvellous." Turning to me, he added, "You can bear me out, for you also know something of the workings of the native mind, but others will say I am exaggerating." "We must try to convince them," I replied.

Jacobsdal, she insisted on her old servant sleeping in our room, even when I, not being on duty, slept there myself. The Boers considered this arrangement simply revolting. The good, faithful creature lay on the ground between our two beds, attentive to her mistress's slightest gesture, and always with a stick ready to her hand in case of attack. One morning she told us that a man had got in during the night.

"Why didn't you wake us?" her mistress asked.

"He didn't do the *missis* any harm, and the *missis* were sleeping so beautifully! My *missi* is very ill, and the other *missi* is very tired."

Was not this intelligent protection nice? Most white women would have shrieked with terror under such circumstances. The black servant's one thought was to watch the intruder and keep us from being disturbed.

When I think that these people have been despoiled and enslaved by a set of ignorant and rapacious peasants; when I think that the whole of Europe is wrath with England because she has applied the *lex talionis* to the Boers; when I think of all the foolish remarks, lies, and ignorant assertions I shall hear and read when I return home, I tell myself that Truth is dead and Justice dying.

This morning the Boers bombarded Warrenton for some hours, The English did not reply, How long is this kind of thing going to last, I wonder?

"When the English fire you keep quiet," I say to the Boers, "and when you begin they don't reply. This is a queer kind of war!"

These worthy Boers are in no hurry to fight. They prefer to sit still and smoke their pipes. "*Onz ess moug*" ("We are tired"), they say, which is quite natural on the part of a lot of poor devils kept at the *laagers* while the big farmers escape by paying bribes in the shape of cattle, horses, and food.

I had a queer patient to watch last night. Usually we do not take typhoid cases, for fear of infecting the beds intended for wounded, but Dr. Weber, who is most humane, could not refuse to take this patient in for one night before he was sent on to Christiana. He was a fifteen-year-old soldier (they fight like demons, these youngsters), and had been laid low by the horrible typhoid fever that is ravaging the neighbouring *laagers*. When the doctor handed him over to me, and I had put him to bed, I prepared to wash him all over, in accordance with the elementary principles in such cases, but he would not hear of it. He plunged about like a wild animal, clung to the bedclothes, and curled himself up with desperate energy. We nurses perform the washing of patients almost without thinking, especially during an epidemic such as is in progress here, and the youngster's fright first astonished and then amused me. To use force being the worst possible way to deal with a patient, and having full confidence in my powers, as every nurse should if she loves her profession, I merely remarked inwardly, "You'll have to give in, my boy." Then I said aloud—

"Will you have something to drink, *manneken*?" ("little man").

He fixed his big, feverish, black eyes on me, and gave no answer; but when I put my hand under his neck he offered no resistance, and when I placed the cup to his lips he drank. I then lay down on an empty bed adjoining his, for I was still far from well, and pretended to sleep, so that he could look at me and accustom himself to my face and dress. When I thought the proper time had come, I rose, gave him another drink, and said—

"Can I wash you now? Be a good boy, and let your mother do it for you."

The word "mother" conquered him. It appealed to the gentler side of his young nature, accustomed to maternal tenderness, and the poor little soldier—solitary, ill, abandoned, as he thought, by God and man—gave in, and looked at me with an expression far removed from his former obstinacy.

"Will you let me?" I asked.

"Yes, *Zuster*."

When they came to take him away at daybreak, he was sorry to leave his temporary mother. I thought of his real mother, and the anxiety that must be gnawing at her heart. If she had only known that her child's life was hanging by a thread!

We have just heard that General de Villebois is marching this way. If this be true, it will be delightful, and will considerably simplify matters, there being some friction here. The Russian doctor knows we want to join the Foreign Legion, and we know he wants to have Russian Sisters here. Moreover, I am beginning to have enough of twiddling my thumbs. I did not come here for that.

A Russian nurse has just arrived. She is a young lady of good birth, very intelligent, very well educated, and very prepossessing. I like her because she makes delicious hot rolls, and is indescribably funny. She puts on high boots before she begins to cook. Why? I can't make it out; and when I ask Madame Thouvenot to explain the mystery, she being in the Franco-Russian alliance, she gets angry, and cuts me short. A young Russian medical man from Riga, Dr. Bernhaupt, arrived with the nurse. There are no doldrums when he is about!

April 10.—Our Consul-General at Pretoria, Monsieur Charlier, who is extremely kind and cordial to me, has just forwarded some letters which had been sent to Pretoria. Amongst them is a postcard from Lieutenant Galopaud, dated from Kroonstadt, April 4, and containing the following lines: "I am leaving tonight with my detachment to join General de Villebois.[4] Come as soon as possible. You will be welcome." I should be only too pleased, but how am I to do it? I must get permission from the Medical Committee at Pretoria.

April 15.—We hear that Villebois has been killed, but an hour afterwards the report was denied. It would be so frightfully sad that we cannot, we will not believe it.

April 16.—I have telegraphed to my consul that I cannot waste my time here, that I wish to return to Pretoria, and will pay my own expenses if need be. I make this offer in spite of travelling being so frightfully costly. Six pounds for the thirty-three hours' nightmarish journey by mail is fairly stiff; and then there is the railway fare from Klerksdorp to Johannes- burg, and thence to Pretoria.

The gentlemen of the Medical Committee have been kind enough to admit my right to be sent back, and they undertake to pay all except hotel expenses. I start tomorrow.

There was an inimitably funny scene yesterday between our driver and Madame Thouvenot. She, being very daring, wanted him to help her to wash some linen in the river separating us from the English camp. The black strongly objected, and went through a series of graphic motions with an imaginary rifle, volubly repeating—

"English poum-poum, *Missi*! English poum-poum!"

"No, you idiot," replied the lady, "the English will not poum-poum!"

And they went at it hammer and tongs, both very excited, the one declaring that the English would poum-poum, and the other that the English would not poum-poum. It was comical in the extreme.

These honest blacks are just what I found them at Jacobsdal, that is to say, absolutely devoted to those who are kind to them. When the driver heard that I was leaving, he expressed his regret in a delightful phrase, which, unfortunately, I cannot repeat; and the youngest of the "boys" was quite disappointed because I could not take him to "my country."

---

4. He could not do so, the general having already been killed, and his men made prisoners.

CHAPTER 12

Back to Pretoria

April 21.—General de Villebois is dead. There can be no doubt about it now. I had only spoken to him once, but the news of his death saddened me as only the loss of an old and very dear friend could have done. In imagination I saw him again, with his graceful, fascinating manners, and his keen, clever face lit up by a kind smile as he uttered the flattering words—"If I have to be nursed, may it be by you!" Alas! I was far away when he fell, and, mortally wounded as he was, all my efforts would I have failed to bring him back to life, no nurse, however devoted, being able to perform miracles. Still, had I been there, pious hands would have closed his eyes, and deep and genuine mourning would have followed him to his last resting-place.

Many a time at Jacobsdal have I driven to the cemetery with a coffin bumping up and down in the cart, and hitting me in the back. Often there was no coffin for the poor remains, and I have had to confine myself to sewing them in a blanket. I have rendered these offices, and said a last prayer at the graveside without, I confess, feeling any particular sorrow. I was doing no more than it was my duty to do as a nurse in watching to the last over the body entrusted to my care, but in this case it would have been different. Oh, why was I not there? Judging by all that was told me, this man was a real hero—not the magnified creation of legend and imagination, but an example of pure and genuine heroism, such as France ought to be proud of; a man whom she should mourn as one of the noblest of her sons.

How came it that he, a general, was killed in a skirmish? How came it that an officer of his rank, and a foreigner to boot, was reconnoitring in a country unknown to him? These are questions which naturally occur to anyone. A Belgian, in whom I have the utmost confidence, says he was informed by an official that the general was acting under orders sent to him direct by the Government. I have ceased to wonder at anything, but this would amount to murder. It is a fact, however, that the Boers hold the lives of foreigners very cheap. When the definite announcement of General de Villebois' death reached me, and I spoke of the event as "frightful" to a Boer general, he replied, "Yes, it's a pity," in very much the same tone he would have used in saying, "The sun is setting." To think that a hero's life was sacrificed for such brutes!

Supposing, for the sake of argument, that the order in question was actually given by the Government, why did the general obey it? The problem is insoluble, and, in spite of all my efforts, I cannot drive away the idea that had already taken hold of me at Bloemfontein: "Was he not seeking death? Was not this hero a martyr?"[1] Will the memory of this man, who has fallen on foreign soil and given his life to defend a country not his own, be cherished as it should be by those for whom he died, or will ingratitude and neglect be his lot? It were better not to linger over a question so full of cruel doubt, and I prefer to pass on with a last tribute from the humble nurse to the illustrious dead.[2]

My return from Fourteen Streams in company with Dr. Bernhaupt was marked by a variety of incidents, some comic and some disagreeable. To begin with, nine of us were crammed into a coach intended for six, and, of course, when the doctor tried to put me into a seat on which it was possible to sit down—the others compelled the unhappy occupant to elevate his knees towards his nose—the other men told him it was taken. On the way, the doctor was obliged to

---

1. The version most generally accredited, and admitted to be possible, even by some of the Boers, was that the general had been betrayed by the "natives"; that he had been deceived as to the distance he had to travel, and went on too adventurously, although his horses were already tired, with the result that they gave out when the English were sighted. I merely record this version without comment
2. On my way back to Europe I made the acquaintance of Baron ran D., a retired Dutch officer, now living in Paris. He reached the Transvaal—in March, I think—to join General de Villebois, and was asked to undertake the duty of obtaining certain articles which had belonged to the deceased. He told me many instances of the politeness and respect with which he was received by the enemy; of the praise they bestowed on the French general, and how greatly they deplored his death; how admirably they behaved throughout the interview, and how fully they appreciated the sacred and delicate nature of the envoy's mission. His disappointment was great when he returned from the English camp. He had brought back certain rather cumbrous articles which he thought would please some of the Boers, but they did not even thank him, and merely remarked diadainfully, "Oh, we've got that already." Sweet people!

bestow a piece of his mind on two Boers who had mistaken me for a pillow, one of them having rested his head on my shoulder, and the other lying against my back.

"Can't you behave properly to a *Zuster?*" the doctor exclaimed in disgust

But he made no impression. The Boers have a profound contempt for European women, and especially for a nurse, whom they regard as a paid servant.

We left Fourteen Streams at 3 p.m., and reached Christiana, where we stopped for supper, in the evening. Here a comical incident, not unmixed with tragedy, helped to relieve the tedium of the journey. When I returned to my seat in the coach, I found two English prisoners sitting behind me. I was surprised to see them wearing ordinary civilian clothing, and questioned them. They told me that they had lived in the neighbourhood for a considerable time, and that they had just been taken prisoners because they would not undertake to fight against their own countrymen. They also said they had been detained at Christiana three days, and were so uncomfortable that they were only too glad to be sent to Pretoria.

While we were talking, a noisy and unseemly altercation began between the Boer general, L., who was travelling with us, and the deputy *landdrost* of Christiana, a Hollander. The general objected to the prisoners going, and the local official retorted that he would take care they did go. A volley of bad language followed, leading up to a terrific row, accompanied by frenzied shouting, shaking of fists and defiant juxtaposition of noses and bodies—all very tremendous, laughable, and disgusting. The Boer having accused the Hollander of blasphemy and want of religion, the Hollander retorted that his religion was as good as the other man's, and that he was just as full of it as the Boer. So they juggled with the name of God and religion until they remembered the prisoners, and then the dispute began afresh, each adversary swearing he had strict orders to carry out. Finally they went to see the *landdrost*, who decided for the general, and the two unlucky Englishmen, outwardly calm but inwardly raging, had to give up their seats to the former occupants, and clear out of the vehicle.

After this *intermezzo* we resumed our journey, and made no more stoppages except to change mules. Here I may remark that few things are more amusing than a mule's delight when his harness is taken off. I have a vivid recollection of going to one of the Jacobsdal *laagers* to fetch a typhoid patient in a German Red Cross ambulance-waggon drawn by eight mules. They had done no work for a fortnight, and were simply wild and brimming over with life and fun. They danced, they jumped, they bounded like horses, and when the driver gave them their heads they dashed off at a frenzied pace, and rattled us along in grand style. Amusing little animals, but rather treacherous; if ever you have the honour of an introduction to a mule, take care, and look out for kicks.

To return to my journey. During the first night, which was horribly cold, our mules were suddenly seized with a desire to play us a trick. Taking advantage, it may be, of momentary somnolence on the part of the driver, our eight mules darted off the road, and tore across the fields, bumping our conveyance about in a style that can easily be imagined, and hurling us in all directions. The driver very cleverly jumped from his box, caught the leaders by their heads and stopped them, for which he was rewarded by a volley of Transvaal Billingsgate from the general. The gallant officer's voice was tremulous—with emotion, let us say.

"My goodness," I remarked to Dr. Bernhaupt, "the general has had a bad fright!"

"*Schön, schön*," was all he replied.

This word, which in itself means nothing particular, was in great favour with my companion, and the variety of humorous meanings it acquired from him was a constant source of amusement to me. His *schön* implied irony, resignation, and suppressed mirth. He was a *pince-sans-rire* in combination with a philosopher, and *schön* was his medium both for *blague* and for resignation. He was, however, a philosopher of only twenty-five, full of vitality and animal spirits, and having a healthy craving for fun. We were well met, for I had arrears of laughter to work off after my trying time at Fourteen Streams. *Schön* recurred on all sorts of occasions; when we were in danger of being upset, when we were exposed for hours to heavy rain, and when the Boers passed an apparently inexhaustible bottle of whisky round and round.

"They have plenty of whisky to fuddle themselves with," I remarked to my companion, "but there was none at Jacobsdal to revive the poor typhoid patients."

"*Schön, schön!*" replied Dr. Bernhaupt, with a discreet smile, implying, "Why trouble yourself over what you cannot prevent, and why wonder at anything here?" Why indeed!

We plodded on all night and through the next day, not reaching Klerksdorp till one o'clock in the morning. I shall never forget the last few hours of this journey. Never, I hope, shall I suffer such agonies of impotent rage. In the darkness, our driver's lamp having gone out, I wept, and bit my apron with ever-increasing anguish. I thought of waking Dr. Bernhaupt, but decided that it would never do to involve him in difficulties with a brute holding high rank. It would place him in too risky a position in regard to the authorities at Pretoria, and it is not my way to make an ill return for friendship, or even good-fellowship. When I told him next day what had occurred, he scolded me severely for not waking him, and insisted on making a complaint at Pretoria, but to this I would not consent. Nevertheless, that which I would not say at Pretoria, and cannot relate here, I am ready to give in evidence before the Central Committee of the Geneva Red Cross, to which organization I, having been admitted to the Transvaal branch, belong. It were, perhaps, well that these things should be known.

At Klerksdorp we ate a hasty meal, and I went to bed at half-past one. As I had to catch a train for Pretoria at six o'clock the same morning, and as my kind and cordial travelling companion had to await the coming of the head of his ambulance, we said goodbye; but I was so exhausted that I did not hear the knock at my door, and slept right on until the dinner-bell rang at six o'clock in the evening. When I entered the dining-room, Dr. Bernhaupt greeted me with a "*Schön, schön!*" I fully expected it. He told me that the hostess, who was very uneasy about me, had gone to my room three times, but could not find it in her heart to wake me. At six o'clock next morning—there was only one train a day—we left for Johannesburg, whence my lively companion took train for Kroonstadt, and I for Pretoria. We shall, doubtless, never meet again.

I am compelled to take some rest here with, my kind compatriots, who have made a second sweet home for me. I was completely worn out by privations and the physical suffering due to my carriage accident. It was exasperating to be laid on the shelf, but there was no help for it. I had to accept my fate with as much resignation as I could muster, until it should become more clement. We were all walking over life on a tight-rope, with hope as a balancing-pole.

I have recovered. I have sought employment and found it.

I was told that Colonel Maximoff, who had come from Russia to fight for the Boers, had taken over the command of General de Villebois' Foreign Legion; [2] that he wanted a small field ambulance to

2. This was incorrect The Legion was broken up after the death of General de Villebois. Maximoff was in command of a Hollander corps.

follow the Legion wherever it went; and that an offer to form such an ambulance had been made to a foreign medical man, but declined. I requested our consul, who knew Colonel Maximoff, to write to him on my behalf. The colonel replied at once through his secretary that I could come, and that I was to make arrangements with a doctor of the Russian ambulance to follow him to the front. The colonel himself was under treatment at the Russian and Dutch hospital at Kroonstadt for four wounds he had received only a few days before.

The Medical Committee approved of my plan, gave me a pass, and authorized me to telegraph to them for any supplies I might require. I obtained my passport, and started at 8 p.m., arriving at Kroonstadt next morning at eleven. I went to the hospital, expecting to find my wounded officer, but he had left for Pretoria! *Schön, schön!* as Dr. Bernhaupt would have said. I telegraphed to my consul, informing him that I was returning, and asking him to try to clear up the mystery. On my way back to the station I was accosted by a Dutch gentleman, the manager of the Russian and Dutch ambulance.

"*Zuster*," he said, "I am told you are going back to Pretoria. Is that correct?"

"Quite," I replied.

"Would you like to help one of our *Zusters*? She is going to Pretoria with an ambulance-train full of sick and wounded."

I accepted willingly, and was soon introduced to the Dutch nurse—a charming girl who knew her business well—to the Dutch doctor on duty, who was the chief surgeon of the Kroonstadt hospital, and finally to a third Hollander, secretary of the ambulance-train department, but formerly holding an important post under the Government. His name was Van der Heyden, and I record it here in order that he may have the credit he deserves for his admirable self-sacrifice, his skill, kindness to the sick and wounded, tact, and indulgence towards the nurses under his orders. He was modest, too, and gave us a large share of the credit for what the ambulance accomplished. He told us the daily and hourly vexations he had to endure, and the obstacles that were placed in his way. Many of his so-called helpers were Boer ladies who would remark "*Onz moug*" ("I am tired") after half an hour's work, and young persons who meant well, but had not the slightest notion of nursing. He was obliged to put up with this kind of thing because the Medical Committee insisted on his taking Mr. A.'s wife, Mr. B.'s wife, Mr. B.'s daughter, Mr. C.'s niece, and so on.

"Sometimes," he said, "I have had ten of them trying to manage what you two have just done without any fuss at all. One girl made five journeys in the train, and did not know where the dispensary was! They were constantly calling either the doctor or me from our work."

"The patients must have been very badly attended to," my companion remarked.

"I should think they were, *Zusters*," he replied, with honest indignation; "but you cannot refuse anything to a lady whose husband or father is rich and influential."

It is the same story everywhere, I thought; the humble and the sufferer are invariably sacrificed to interest or vanity.

We left Kroonstadt at about noon with forty-three patients, of whom thirty-three were wounded and the other ten were typhoid-fever or gastroenteritis cases. Our train consisted of two large ambulance-cars containing two rows of upper and two of lower berths on each side; another car, divided into compartments for the doctors, assistants, dispensary, and Mr. Van der Heyden, and a fourth car used as a store. At the end of the train was the kitchen, where two Dutch volunteer cooks managed to concoct quite a variety of appetizing dishes. These ambulance-cars are simply wonderful, but the jolting makes the nurse's work anything but easy, and the difficulty is much greater in the case of the upper berths, she being obliged to stand on the edge of the lower bunk and hang on with one hand.

There were some funny incidents, of course. A large bowl of gruel, left on a stool by an attendant, was upset by an unusually bad bump, and fell on a patient, smothering him with the liquid, much to the delight of the others. One of them exclaimed, "He's had enough to eat for today, *Zuster*." We had great trouble to clean the unlucky patient.

This train is a perfect Tower of Babel. Our patients include Boers, Germans, Dutch, Irish, Americans, two English officers (prisoners), and a Frenchman, who was delighted to find that his nurse could talk to him in his own language. During the afternoon he broke put into the Marseillaise, and I was obliged to ask him to reflect on the appalling consequences which would ensue if every patient followed the example, and struck up his own national anthem. He admitted the justice of the observation. Poor fellow, though he was so far away from his country, it was all the nearer to his heart.

My fellow-nurse proposed that we should divide the night into watches, and I took the first, but had not the heart to wake her when the time came. There was little merit in this, it being easy to accustom one's self to night duty when there are many patients to be attended to, whereas, if only two or three beds are occupied, the nurse is liable to go to sleep. The work was, nevertheless, difficult in this train, the cars not being connected by a vestibule, so that we were compelled to jump from one car to another, often with our hands full.

Having resolved to tell the whole truth and nothing but the truth, it is my duty to note here that the surgical arrangements on the ambulance-train left something to be desired. These defects were inexplicable, seeing how admirably the train, as a whole, was organized.

For instance, during the night two patients were seized with violent pains. To give them relief, a certain surgical instrument wag absolutely necessary. My case being with my other luggage, I applied to the doctor on duty and to the secretary. The one replied that the hospital ought to supply such instruments, and the other that the doctor ought to provide himself with them. The end of it was that the nurse had to do the best she could to relieve the patients, who were suffering such agonies that they kept all the others awake.

Early in the morning we were informed that only the wounded could be received at Pretoria, and that we should have to go back with our sick to Johannesburg. The order, it seems, was sent off too late, and our secretary was rightfully indignant. We reached Pretoria about six o'clock, and there I witnessed an exciting scene in dumb show.

One of the two English officers—both strong, handsome fellows, about thirty years of age, from India—had a fractured leg, and could not leave his bed; the other, whose arm was broken, was able to get up. While the train was standing in the station at Pretoria, they saw a plank sloping to the ground from their car, and I caught them exchanging glances full of meaning. The lame man's look was decidedly mischievous; the other's was full of determination and hope. I realized at once that he meant to escape. At the same instant they both looked at me, and I felt that they knew I had guessed their thoughts. I could not repress a smile, and turned quietly away, hoping the poor fellow might succeed, but feeling convinced that he would soon be caught.

When I was a little girl my sympathies were always with Punch against the policeman. I still have a horror of everything I take to be an abuse of strength or of power, and it would always have pleased me to facilitate the escape of a prisoner, whether Boer or English. Pity was the only feeling that guided me for the moment, but it soon occurred to me that my fellow-nurse, being a Dutchwoman, might perhaps be severely reprimanded if one of our prisoners escaped. I therefore said to her—

"Just look at those Englishmen. One of them is preparing to escape. I should be only too pleased to shut my eyes to it, but what do you intend to do?"

Her high-spirited reply was, "We are nurses, and not jailers."

We walked away, watching them out of the corner of our eyes. How my heart beat! The prisoner walked nonchalantly towards the door without appearing to hurry, looked outside, walked down the plank and disappeared. As soon as he was out of sight my colleague suddenly remembered her responsibility, and also that, to a Dutchwoman such as herself, an Englishman must be an enemy.

"We really cannot let him go like that," she said. "Come with me and stop him, *Zuster*."

"No," I replied, "not I."

I was terribly disappointed, and continued, "Sister, I will say I was alone when he got off."

"No, don't do that," she replied. "Let us each take the responsibility of our own actions."

"Well, then, go," I said, "I shall stay here."

She in her turn disappeared. The injured officer looked anxiously at me, and while I indicated my doubts by a shake of the head, I saw her returning, soon followed by the prisoner, who had found out at once that all attempt to escape was useless. Alas! the wings of hope had soon been clipped.

My duties finished at Pretoria, but as the train remained there for two hours I had time to do my errands, and as I wished to help the other nurse up to the last with the work we had undertaken together, I promised her I would return. It seemed as though I should have to wait an eternity before obtaining a cab, though the youthful cabbies were shouting, "Hi, *Missi*, a cab?" I only wished I could get one, but a crowd of Boers who had just got out of the train pounced upon all the cabs, and gave me no chance. Finally one of the Boers, more thoughtful than the rest, said to me—

"*Zuster*, would you like us to take a carriage together, and I will drive you where you have to go?"

"I shall be very glad to do so," I said.

When we were in the vehicle I explained that I was in a hurry, having to join the ambulance-train.

He was sorry for the cab incident, and said, "People are not always nice to the Sisters here."

"No," I replied. "But do you know who are the best in your country? The women, the boy soldiers, and old men."

"Old men like me, I suppose!"

"You are not very old, but you are as good as an old person."

He laughed heartily, and seemed pleased. Then, becoming serious again, he said—

"Ah, *Zuster*, things are going very badly, and we are sick of it."

"Yes," I said. "If this wretched war could only be ended, it would be well for both sides. It is time it was."

"The English are men like ourselves, *Zuster*."

"Certainly, poor things!"

It was always pleasant to me to have evidence of the almost entire absence of hatred between the "enemies." More and more I became convinced that it was a conflict between two Governments, and not a war between two peoples.

Upon arriving at my destination, I paid my share to this good Boer. He helped me to get out my packages, we shook hands, and he went on his way.

The cab tariff here is very peculiar, and sometimes very dear (it is always the same, the price not having risen since the war)—seven shillings the hour. For a single drive from one place to another you pay according to the number of occupants; thus, if you are alone you pay one shilling, and if four, four shillings. As to the tip, two-pence will quite startle the driver, especially if he be a black.

Later on, I paid a visit to Colonel Maximoff, who was naturally annoyed that I had had an unnecessary journey.

"My time was not wasted, I assure you," I said. "I have found work, and must be off again immediately."

"For good?"

"No; I shall come back this evening, and then I shall be at your disposal."

He then told me that he expected to return as soon as possible to the Dutch corps under his orders near Kroonstadt, and we agreed to meet next evening at the station.

After this interview I returned to the ambulance-train. When it reached Johannesburg, I experienced one of those delights—the sweetest, purest, and profoundest in existence—that nurses alone know and appreciate. Some Jewish bearers came to fetch our typhoid patients, a few of whom were also wounded. When the bearers were lifting them I trembled, fearing the bearers might move our dear patients too roughly; but, to my surprise, they handled them as gently as a woman would have done. When I saw them set off with the first litter down the inclined plane, I exclaimed, "Gently, gently!"

A voice replied, "Don't be afraid!" And, indeed, we were soon reassured, and admired the extraordinary cleverness of these young men. They had an easy knack, which older hospital attendants might have envied, of raising the stretcher so that the patient remained in a horizontal position.

The voice which had said, "Don't be afraid," asked, "Are you satisfied now, Sister?"

We expressed our admiration and complete satisfaction, and were told that the entire expenses of this corps were borne by one person, the one to whom we were speaking. He, of course, was a Jew.

"It is very good of you," said the Dutch woman.

"Ah," said I, "if there were more generous, sympathetic people like you, what a good place the world would be!"

He seemed so much touched, this good man, that I imagined that the Boers had neglected to thank him from the beginning of the war. One can't think of everything!

When our last patients were out of the train, we began to put things straight. To change sheets and pillow-cases, and air the mattresses of forty-three beds, after being on the go for twenty-four hours, was no easy task. At length all was finished, and then we had our reward.

Mr. Van der Heyden took us round the town, and, believe me, we were a gay party; but after an hour's walking I was in such pain on account of my boots, which were down at heel and twisted my feet, that I demanded a conveyance of some kind, either one of the light vehicles drawn by a black, or a carriage. It was very difficult to find anything of the kind; so difficult, in fact, that we declared we should have to forcibly dislodge the first person we saw in anything on wheels. We even made believe to do so. I can see it now, the negro driver's delight when he saw through the joke, and the good lady's alarm! She was divided between fear and amusement, and her face looked like one of those India-rubber doll-heads that a child squeezes up in its hand.

Eventually a miserable *Rosinante*, drawing a caravan that Noah would not have allowed in his ark, came up. We got in, and began a wildly exciting drive. Our Jehu was not only unskilful but intoxicated, and after running us on to the sidewalks and colliding with everything he possibly could, he tried to drive into the public gardens, but capsized us against the railings. We were so exhausted with laughter when we returned to the train that our chief treated us to a glass of delicious Burgundy and a few biscuits, after which he went off to draw up his report, and we were able to get a little sleep.

Mr. Van der Heyden and the Dutch Sister returned to Kroonstadt with the ambulance-train, she to rejoin her hospital and he because he was seldom away from the train. As I was bound for Pretoria, which lay in the opposite direction, we had to take leave of each other. This we did with many regrets, and hoped that we should make another journey together. Before finally leaving me, Mr. Van der Heyden took me to the train to see me off. Every seat in the first-class carriages was already occupied.

"Is there no room for the *Zuster?*" he asked.

No reply.

He tried again. "The *Zuster* is very tired," he said. "She has been travelling ever since the night before last, and she has been on train-duty since yesterday morning."

"No," a voice replied; "there's no room here."

Observing how great my companion's annoyance was, I begged him to say no more. He protested against my travelling in a third-class carriage; but I made light of it, inwardly reflecting that the Boers' third-class carriage seats were less hard than their own hearts.

After a last hand-shake I climbed into the car, proceeded to settle myself as well as I could—the compartment being crammed, not only with passengers, but with all sorts of objects, even coops of hens— and the train started. My travelling companions were a motley crew. There were well-to-do citizens who had been crowded out of better carriages, peasants, townsfolk and combatants. I soon noticed a rather young married couple, accompanied by a little black maidservant who carried a child. The lady wore a black silk dress, trimmed with sky-blue and with black lace that was a marvel of pretentious ugliness. Her husband, in obedience to a few words from her, dived into a bag and brought out a cushion, or rather a pillow, trimmed with torn embroidery, and attempted to place it under the head of his spouse, but she repelled it.

Then her husband proceeded to perform a series of gymnastic feats, turning his shoulders, raising his knees, and balancing himself in a dangerously unsteady way on the edge of the seat, so that his wife could lie comfortably with her head on his legs. All this time he held the cushion clasped to his bosom. Three times I thought they had hit on the required position, and three times they resumed their contortions, in imminent danger of falling off the seat. The wrigglings of these two beings were almost sublimely ridiculous, but the indifference of the other passengers, who seemed to think it the most natural thing in the world, was still more extraordinary. At one time I was obliged to hide my laughter under my cape. When I looked out again, the problem had been solved; the lady was peaceably reposing, and the gentleman's limbs were contorted into attitudes suggestive of a atone demon from a Gothic cathedral.

The black nurse and her charge provided me with amusement of another kind. Any one might have thought these spectacles had been organized by Uncle Paul for my amusement, although I was travelling with a free pass. The little *blackamoor* produced an orange from her pocket, and proceeded to lick it all over, and scratch it with her wizened little monkey fingers. Next she contemplated it, and turned it round and round very much as a monkey does with nut. Then she began to lick and scratch it again, after which she poked her finger through the rind and sucked the juice. This kept her busy for some time.

Next she began to shake the orange—possibly because there was no more juice to be got out of it—and wave it from right to left, and up and down, and backwards and forwards, at first slowly, but gradually faster and faster; and while she waved the orange with one arm, the other caused the baby to describe similar movements. The rolling and pitching grew so appalling that I felt myself in danger of sea-sickness. Accordingly, I lay down on the floor, with my bag for a pillow and my woollen cloak as a mattress, and slept, having, thank Heaven, two hours available for rest.

On reaching Pretoria I was accosted by a young man in a state of considerable worry, who said he was very glad to see me. I replied that I had not the honour of his acquaintance. He explained that he had telegraphed to Johannesburg for a nurse to attend to his mother, and he supposed I had come for that purpose. I replied that I had not, and that I was the only nurse who had come by the train. I nevertheless offered to stay with his mother that night if he could find no one else. He made no reply, but rushed off to find the other nurse. Perhaps he thought I was trying to deprive a rival of a good billet, nurses being very well paid here. He was an English-speaking Boer. I waited for a short time, and then went on my way. I regretted it afterwards; but I was really a perfect wreck, and, to crown all, I had to walk home, all the cabs being taken. Next evening Colonel Maximoff and I started for Kroonstadt.

CHAPTER 13

Kroonstadt Abandoned

We reached Kroonstadt on the following afternoon. There was a long stoppage on the way, and all sorts of rumours were current as to its cause. For a long time it was believed that the English were coming. As there were a great many Boers got up like Tartarin de Tarascon in the Alps, Maximoff said, "We are all armed, and if the English come, we can pick off a good many of them."

It was amusing to see the terror with which the Boers received this idea. The colonel did not, as a rule, admit that the Boers were wanting in courage, but this time there was no help for it.

When we reached Kroonstadt, we were told that the English were quite near. In the evening we slept at the hospital. I was offered a bed in the Sisters' quarters; and as the colonel occupied a room at the other end of the hospital, I knew nothing of his doings, I was therefore not a little surprised when I rose next morning, rather late, to hear that he had started on horseback at seven o'clock. Someone, professing to be very well informed, added that the colonel would not come back. I began to think that this kind of treatment was rather peculiar, but I resolved to await developments.

Time passed on, and the colonel, like Malbrook, did not return. I spent a very disagreeable time, and the Dutch doctor who took the place of the chief surgeon in charge of the ambulance train behaved very badly to me. Holland does not love Belgium, and cannot forgive her for having regained her independence; but all the Dutch whom I encountered here were, with this one exception, very kind and obliging. I merely mention the case to show how many questions still remain to be settled by the Geneva Red Cross, and also to remind other nurses who may read these pages that they should always stand up for their rights, and not allow themselves to be discouraged.

This doctor asked me what I intended to do. I replied that I should wait for the colonel.

"Suppose he does not come back?" the doctor asked.

"He is sure to come," I replied.

"You know nothing about it, *Zuster*," the Dutchman growled irritably.

I stared at him, and did so with all the less difficulty as he never looked anyone in the face. He was a thin, bilious man, with a halo of long, fuzzy hair round his head, and his appearance was that of a raw countryman from some remote Dutch village. No doubt he thought his little brief authority made it his duty to disregard politeness.

Some waggons were passing at the time, and he said, "Get in one of those, and go and find something to do in one of the *laagers*."

"How do you know," I retorted, "that those waggons are going to the *laagers*? And if they are, should I find anything to do?"

"I don't know anything about it," he replied; "but I warn you that all I can do is to give you a meal or two, and then you will have to shift for yourself."

At this, moment the chief medical officer of the Orange Free State Red Cross arrived on the scene. He it was who had sent me to Jacobsdal, and had been so kind to me when I passed through Bloemfontein, both going and coming. I thought I should find a protector in him, and explained the circumstances; but instead of welcoming me as before, he showed no signs of interest in the matter, feeling, no doubt, that he would best please the Boer ladies by giving me a cold reception. When I pointed out that the Pretoria Medical Committee had sent me to join Colonel Maximoff's ambulance, the Orange Free State doctor declared that the Pretoria Committee had nothing to do with it, and the other medico added that Colonel Maximoff had no right to choose any of the nurses.

Much to the dismay of the Boer ladies, who had been perpetually asking me when I was going to start, I thanked the doctors for their information, and quietly told them I should stay where I was. I had decided in my own mind that, if Maximoff did not come back, I should wait until the English reached Pretoria, and then I should be sure of assistance and respect.

I soon found that I had been well advised in holding out. In the afternoon Maximoff's secretary, a Pretoria Hollander, who spoke French very well, and was one of the State Secretary's attaches, called on me, and was very indignant when I told him of the attempts that had been made to get rid of me. He assured me that Maximoff was sure to return, inasmuch as he himself had been ordered to wait for the colonel. I replied that I thought so too, but I had been so badgered by the Hollander's amiable countryman that I had begun to doubt.

While we were talking, groups of horsemen began to collect in front of the hotel, eagerly questioning one another. It appeared from what they said that things were going very badly with the Boers. There was nothing less than a general stampede, and Kroonstadt would be abandoned without a blow being struck. When the Boers said this the Hollanders began to abuse them. They had had enough, they declared, of doing all the fighting and having all their friends killed, while the Boers were running away and giving up the best positions; to which the Boers replied that as the Hollanders wanted the war, they had better keep it up. "As for us," the Boers concluded, "*Onz geft op*" ("we give up").

Every quarter of an hour a fresh and contradictory report arrived. First we heard that the English were already close to the town, then that they were still a long way off, or would not be here for two days, or that they would be sighted within an hour, and so on. All the time bodies of fugitives were passing through the town, sitting dejectedly on their tired horses.

Five o'clock.—I have just been told a terrible thing. The mere act of recording such ignominious conduct is painful to me, but nevertheless it must be done. The ambulance-train was waiting, orders having been given to clear the hospitals out, so that the patients should not be made prisoners. Before all the patients could be put on the train, a number of terrified Boers swarmed on to it—it being the last train to leave here—and refused to move, swearing that they had as much right there as the patients. All they cared about, these heartless cowards, was to save their own precious skins. It mattered not to them that, they were taking the places of their comrades who, having already shed their blood for their country, were entitled to consolation and relief. It must have been a repulsive spectacle. If I had been on duty in this train, and could have found a weapon, I would have used it, without the slightest hesitation or regret, on these wretches.

I have been called to see a wounded man just brought in. He was terribly injured about the head, throat, and chest, and the blood was trickling out from beneath the bandages. Although he was evidently unconscious, he appeared to be suffering agonies. It was just as if a fierce struggle were going on between the dying man and some invisible being. The sight was so dreadful that no one who had any affection for the poor fellow could have endured it. His gasps were like the panting of a steam-engine, and the rattling in his throat reminded me of the crushing of stones in a mill. Why are we not allowed to end the sufferings of these poor fragments of humanity, death being an absolute certainty in such cases?

The same reflection had already occurred to me at Jacobsdal, where the typhoid patients were buried before they were cold. Why were we refused the permission we asked to open a vein in the wrist? I admit that even this precaution would not have made it absolutely certain that the patient was dead before he was put under the ground, but it would certainly have greatly reduced the chances of his being alive. I am convinced that in war large numbers of men are buried who would survive if they had an opportunity.

Six o'clock.—Colonel Maximoff has just returned, and has sent for me. His four wounds are very painful, and he is completely worn out, having passed almost the entire day on horseback or going about with President Steyn. He speaks of the President with a depth of emotion such as he does not usually betray. The colonel, in fact, is a man of action, and his manners savour somewhat of the camp. He is a believer in the poetry of war, and says he likes nothing better than to hear the whistling of bullets and the thunder of cannon; and, in fact, when he indulges in recollections of his service with Skobeleff, the handsome "white *cuirassier,*" his face lights up, and he becomes a poet inspired by the noise of war.

This Russian soldier is a new and interesting psychological study. He certainly has not the attractiveness of Villebois, although his bearing is open and gentlemanly enough. He gave me the impression that his manners were somewhat artificial and might prove to be only skin deep. What he was as a man is of little consequence, especially as his sufferings had made him somewhat irritable. He would not admit that the Boers were wanting in courage, and yet it was his fate to see them run away, time after time, instead of staying to fight it out. His character as a soldier alone can be of any importance here; and in this respect he was faultless. He was brave even to rashness, as all his men told me, while he delighted in relating incidents which showed the indomitable bravery of his Dutch followers.

One instance will show that there was no exaggeration on either side. At ——[1] the colonel ordered his men to attack a position. They

1. I cannot find the name of this locality in my notes.

hesitated, thinking the attempt was sure to fail. The colonel, exclaiming, "You'll see I am right," dashed forward, and his men followed him. The colonel was wounded in four places: in the foot, shoulder, ear, and temple. (This wound was decidedly curious from the surgical point of view. It was caused by a bullet, but looked exactly like a sword-cut.) This fourth wound, on the temple, was by far the most serious, and when he received it, the colonel fell like a log, while his men gathered round him, and opened a sharp fire to protect him. The incident shows the high qualities of the officer as well as those of his men.

What the colonel told me of Steyn, his sufferings and his alternation of hope and despair, was absolutely painful. Steyn is the noblest, finest, and most disinterested figure in the Transvaal war. He is the incarnation of bravery, self-sacrifice, and stainless honesty. He, at any rate, has not filled his pockets with bribes from the country he is now fighting. His conscience is clear, his hands are clean; he is a *savant*, his heart is in the right place, and he is as brave as a lion. This was the man who, after pouring out all his eloquence on the hordes of bandits who were betraying their country by abandoning one of the very finest positions, cried like a child, and told them their country was holding out its arms to them in despair, like a mother to her children.

But nothing was to be got out of these unintelligent creatures of impulse, guided only by their good pleasure, and having nothing but a viscera where the heart should be. No one can conceive what this man must have suffered. In fact, no such conception could be possible to anyone who had not some measure of his sublime and superhuman patriotism. The name of Steyn will always remain in my mind as a symbol of everything noble and great. How I regret I never had an opportunity of seeing him! At Pretoria it never occurred to me to go out of my way for a look at old President Kruger. The two presidents had absolutely distinct positions in the esteem and admiration of the masses, and were spoken of in very different tones.[2]

---

2. These lines were written in May, and now (December) Steyn has attained unexplored heights of heroism. He stands out in brilliant relief against the dark background of war, with Botha and De Wet as his attendant satellites. These three men have practically monopolized the Boer courage with which it is sought to throw a halo over the entire nation. Undoubtedly the handful of men still in the field and electrified by such irresistible leaders, make up for a great deal of cowardice; but it is none the less true that the Boers gave up the strongest positions between Jacobsdal and Pretoria, such as Bloemfontein, Kroonstadt, and Johannesburg, without showing fight. I therefore ask any fair-minded person to tell me what foundation there is for the stories of the Boers' fierce and indomitable courage. (Continued next page).

A Russian doctor and myself were talking to Maximoff, who was lying upon his bed, when suddenly there was a fearful noise, indescribably loud and sharp. We instinctively rushed towards the door, convinced that the entire hospital was being blown up.

"It's an eight-gun battery gun in action," remarked the colonel.

I had never heard anything like it either at Jacobsdal or Fourteen Streams. We waited a few moments in great perplexity, and then someone came to tell us that the last of the Boers who remained in the locality before taking flight had blown up the railway bridge. It was the only thing they could think of. They had considerately waited until President Steyn had gone away, so that he was, at any rate, spared regret for the destruction of this splendid piece of engineering work.

The English continuing their advance, I remarked to the colonel that it was time to leave. He exclaimed—

"Never, never have I run away from an enemy."

"It's not running away," I replied; "it's going away. Do you want the English to have the pleasure of taking you prisoner?"

"I don't care. A few resolute men "

"It is all very well to talk about resolute men," I rejoined, "but you are the only man left in the place. All the others are running away."

At length we decided to go, but the getting off was not so easy. I cannot here relate all the annoying, though laughable, incidents that occurred.

About eight o'clock, an hour and a quarter before the English arrived, we started, the colonel on horseback, his secretary, his "boy," and myself in a kind of dog-cart, into which we had thrown an incalculable number of packages. As for finding room for ourselves, that was

---

At present we are witnessing the useless and painful exhibition that is being made of President Kruger. How can diplomatic questions be settled by sentiment, seeing that war, which is a collective crime against humanity and is inspired by anything but mercy and kindness, is the very essence of man's animalism? Why, then, seek to encourage this old man with false hopes? Why so direct the currents of thought and speech as to exasperate England instead of attempting to conciliate her? Countries are no readier than individuals to admit themselves in the wrong. The misguided ambition of President Kruger's advisers was responsible for the Emperor William's refusal to receive him. The poor old man, borne down with years and sorrows, should have been spared this affront, but neither his age nor the trust he placed in others was respected. He has even lost prestige in the eyes of his own people, to whom he had promised a miracle. He can no longer style them the "chosen people." How greatly he would have gained in dignity had he remained at Pretoria, and how much better would it have been for him to die quietly in the arms of his lifelong companion!

quite a secondary consideration. We had to look forward to enduring these discomforts at least all night, perhaps longer; and the difficulty of the situation was increased by the wretched condition of our two horses, half dead with fatigue and hunger. The Dutch doctor and the Boer ladies wished us *bon voyage* and good luck (which meant not getting peppered by any of the English patrols who were reported to be quite close to us) with all the more sincerity as they were delighted to see us clear out. The colonel took all the nice things they said quite literally, and I responded with the utmost amiability, because these little comedies are very amusing, full of variety, and cost nothing.

CHAPTER 14

The Retreat From Kroonstadt

We had not been five minutes on the road when a somewhat mysterious event happened. Two mounted Boers, who had waited about for some time in front of the hospital while we were making our preparations, without appearing to notice our departure, joined us as we left Kroonstadt and got into the country. They passed our conveyance, went up to the colonel, who was a few horse-lengths ahead of us, placed themselves one on his right and the other on his left, and began a conversation. The colonel speaks German very well, and a great many Boers understood a great part of what he said. A Boer's curiosity is as great as his capacity for lying, and at first I thought these men were simply trying to satisfy their desire to ask questions. Then, how the idea arose I cannot say, I found myself distrusting the appearance and manner of these individuals. Why were they staying here so long after the others had fled? I spoke to the secretary about it, and he had his suspicions also. He suddenly asked them to what laager they belonged. They were visibly confused, stammered, and could not remember the name at once. Neither could they tell us promptly where they were going.

"You are right," remarked the secretary; "there is something queer about these men."

I called the colonel, and told him of the questions we had put to the men. I added—

"I think you had better look out, colonel; these two fellows seem to take rather too much interest in you."

"It certainly looks like it," he replied. "I will tell them there are thirty mounted men coming behind us, and then we shall see what they will do."

The colonel's announcement decidedly disconcerted the two Boers, and he added—

"Travelling is unsafe, and we had better be prepared."

Turning to his secretary, Colonel Maximoff continued—

"I shall load, and you had better do the same."

The click of the two weapons was instantly followed by the noise of horses' hoofs galloping away from us. The two mysterious Boers were off to Kroonstadt.

Maximoff gave a few brief orders to his secretary. Rifles and revolvers were loaded, and it was decided that if an English patrol came near——

I urged the colonel to push on, telling him that my nurse's cap was quite sufficient protection, and that there was plenty of light for it to be seen; but he chivalrously insisted on staying to take care of me, and I gave way.

It was one of those marvellous African nights, , full of a stern grandeur and infinitely sad, infinitely sweet poetry, that seem to etherealize and lift me far above this base, mundane life, to cleanse me from the dust of fratricidal and criminal strife, to make me better, purer, and greater, and to transform me into a nobler essence. Words are too feeble to describe my feelings. The most materialistic of beings could not but ask himself if there is not another life as full of radiant light and serene beauty as this sky and atmosphere. It is but the fleeting beauty of a mirage, yet the impression it creates is worth even the cruel awakening from the dream.

Suddenly an immense sheaf of flames shot up towards the fleecy clouds on the horizon. It grew and spread out into a furious, raging sea of fire.

"Look!" I exclaimed; "Kroonstadt is burning.

"Then the English must be there already," remarked one of my companions.

"Why should they set fire to the town?" I asked. "What is there to show that they have done it?"

We stopped, and the gentlemen, noting the direction of the fire, came to the conclusion that the burning buildings were the forage and goods stores at the railway station. The Boers who blew up the bridge are said to have decided on this conflagration.

"To think," said the secretary, "that the horses have been on half-feed for days to save forage, and now any amount of it is going up in smoke!"

We resume our journey, and plod on with an occasional halt to scrutinize the horizon. Figures appear in the distance, and the colonel is convinced they are English. I warn him that I have no bandages at hand, and that I may have some difficulty in sewing him together if he gets into another fight. After much careful reconnoitring on both sides, the distant horsemen are ascertained to be Boers. The colonel's wounds are causing him great pain, which he cannot hide in spite of his pluck. On we go. The cold is becoming intense. At midnight we sight a camp fire, and ask ourselves the same old question—Boers or English? Maximoff, in spite of our remonstrances, rides off to investigate, calling to us to wait for him.

"It's absurd," I remarked to the secretary, a big, good-natured, red-haired fellow. "If those people are English, he will be fired on."

"So shall we," my companion growled; "and all for nothing,"

"There is no danger," I said. "If I see them coming I shall shout, 'Sister,' as I did to the patrols at Jacobsdal, and they won't fire."

"It isn't the same thing here," he said.

"Look at the colonel," I continued; "he is going straight for those people. There is no doubt about it, he is as bold as a lion, though he's as obstinate as a mule."

We waited and waited, hungry and half frozen, not knowing what had become of our fiery warrior. At last we heard a voice hailing us, but whether it came from a friend or enemy we could not tell. We took our chance and moved forward, the prospect of being turned into stalactites having no charm for us. Our unhappy animals had the utmost difficulty in dragging us across country. The secretary and I were swung about like a French salad. At last we encountered the colonel. He was not in an amiable frame of mind, and it transpired that he had been hailing us for the last ten minutes —just those ten minutes we had spent in waiting for him: but he had good news for us.

"The men round the fire yonder are German volunteers," he said, "and they have asked us to share their food. Come along as fast as you can."

We came along, certainly; but as for doing it quickly, that was quite another affair. We arrived at last, and were most hospitably received by some worthy young men, who gave us delicious hot chicken broth. We took it, sitting round a cheerfully crackling brazier; then we devoured the chickens' legs, wings, and bodies. Our horses, too, had double rations. We chattered and laughed, happy to be warm and have something to eat. Now and then there was a "Ssh!" to keep us quiet whenever anything suspicious was sighted. The German lieutenant, observing that the horses were straying too far away, told his men to halter them carefully. "If you don't, those thieves of Boers will get them," he said. "They steal all they can, the pigs."

Maximoff did not hear the word "*Schwein*." If he had, he would probably have protested. He would never admit that he had been taken in; and yet it is far nobler and grander for a man, as for a nation, to be the dupe rather than the dupee.

But the time had come for us to say goodbye and start. It was hard, because we were with good and pleasant comrades, and also because our senses were somewhat dulled by good cheer and the combined effects of biting cold and the intense heat from the brazier. As for Maximoff, whose muscles had stiffened during the hour and a quarter we had spent in rest, he was in great pain, and it was no easy matter for him even to stand. He thought, at first, he could not go on at all; but at length, after great efforts, he managed to walk a little, and we decided that he should go in the conveyance and give his horse to the secretary.

The moonlight was waning and the landscape was becoming more and more obscure. The colonel drove for a short time, and then handed the reins over to me. When my hands were half frozen, he took another turn; then I relieved him again, and so we continued. His sufferings, however, increased, and suddenly he dropped the reins on my knees.

"I am done for. Sister; I can't keep up any longer," he groaned.

I made a place for him as well as I could among the baggage, with the help of cushions and blankets, he being from this moment my patient, that is to say, a helpless being entrusted to my care. Though lying doubled up in a most uncomfortable position, the poor soldier soon fell asleep, utterly exhausted.

I drove on as best I could, knowing that I should have to do it for several hours. My eyes were never very good in a poor light, and my several months' exposure to the glaring African sun had not by any means improved them. Darkness came on apace, and though the road was hardly visible, through some optical delusion there seemed to be two roads instead of one. Nevertheless I drove on with the fatalism which, in me, takes the place of courage, making bets with myself that I should overturn the whole concern in less than ten minutes. But still we went on, and we did not overturn. My fingers were numb with cold, and the horses were half dead. I love animals, but my patient had to be considered first; and, at any cost, we must reach the station in time. I called our boy, who jumped from his seat and ran beside our horses, slashing their feet and bellies with his whip. This spurred them on for a couple of hundred yards or so, and then their speed slackened again. Every quarter of an hour at least we were obliged to treat them with this disgraceful cruelty. From time to time the whip had no effect on them. What on earth was I to do? I asked myself, with a wounded man and dying horses, and what would happen if the cold overcame me?

Thick darkness, threatening and mysterious, bung over us, when we heard a strange, dull, rumbling, far-away sound. It might have been a hurricane or a mighty waterfall; I had never heard anything exactly like it. I hailed the secretary, but he was no wiser than myself. The noise increased as we drew nearer, and we could soon hear the rolling and creaking of wheels, the trotting of horses, and thousands of voices, talking, whispering, and laughing. They were Boers in retreat from Kroonstadt. I thought of their characteristic phrase, "*Onz geft op*," and my blood boiled. The cowards, the wretches! Here they were laughing and joking and singing while the enemy's heel was on their country's throat! The feeling of nausea and disgust I had already experienced at Jacobsdal and Fourteen Streams seized me again. Flemings, these fellows? No, mere flamingoes.

There was quite an army of them. With their countless carts and waggons they formed an immense compact mass moving through suffocating mountains of dust. From time to time it closed on us so threateningly that I fully expected our conveyance to be crushed to pieces. The colonel's secretary had become separated from us, my patient was still asleep, and I tried to pick my way as best I might so as to postpone as long as possible the process of being reduced to a jelly, which I imagine must be very disagreeable. Occasionally the road broadened out, and we could breathe more freely, literally as well as figuratively. Some Boers greeted me with a "Goodnight, auntie" (the word used by the most amiable among them when addressing a woman whom they do not know). I merely replied "Goodnight," having no desire to enter upon a conversation. Then some of the older men would remark compassionately, "Poor auntie, your horses are very tired"; and others would ask, "Whom have you got there, auntie?" When I told them the wounded man was Maximoff, they repeated the name one to another, and admitted that he had fought well. Then came the usual silly questions, such as, "Are you looking after him?"

"Yes," I replied; "I was to have gone to the front with him, but as you have abandoned Kroonstadt———"

They changed the subject, and one of them asked—

"Are you a *Zuster*, auntie?"

Before I could reply, he struck a match, and said—

"Yes, I see you are."

I could not restrain a laugh. "Did you take me for an English soldier, *fader*?" I asked,

Then the horrible crowding began again, I had to steer like a pilot in a mazy channel, without relaxing my attention for a single instant, and I feared that we should never, never reach our journey's end. But the longest lane has a turning, and at last a faint, pale light, like a vague hope, made its appearance. About three-quarters of an hour later, after a long climb and long crawl downhill, both equally trying to our wretched horses, who had forgotten to die, we caught sight of the station. An immense train, at least three times as long as any I have ever seen in Europe, was there. It had been waiting ever since two o'clock in the morning for some of the fugitives from Kroonstadt, but others from I know not where had taken it by storm.

The corridors as well as the compartments were full of snoring Boers. I had to step over them in search of a corner for my wounded patient, but neither threats nor entreaties had the slightest effect. Not one of them would budge. It was truly cheering to see young and healthy Boers refusing to disturb themselves so that a foreign officer,' wounded in the service of their country, could find a little room in which to lay his bruised and wearied limbs! When I am in charge of a patient I am fiercely indifferent to anything but his well-being, and I left the train in search of some older and better-natured person than these Boers. It was now broad daylight. I wandered from group to group, trying to discover a good-natured face. I found it, and joy! it belonged to a commandant. He was greatly annoyed by what I told him, and said—

"Come with me, *Zuster*. We will soon put that right."

We climbed into the nearest car. He seized a young Boer nearly as big and strong as a tree, and shook him.

"Aren't you ashamed of yourself?" he shouted. "Here's Colonel Maximoff wounded, and yet you won't make room for him or the poor *Zuster* who has brought him here."

Some of the Boers woke and growled out, "*Onz ess moug*" ("we are tired").

"It's six o'clock now, and you've been sleeping here since two," the commandant retorted. "Make room for others."

"Do you think I should interfere with you if you were wounded?" I asked. "I want room on a seat for my patient, and not for myself."

"Not a bit of it, Sister," exclaimed the commandant, who was becoming as fiercely zealous for the wounded man as I was. "You must rest. Now then," he continued, "get up, there!"

At last two or three Boers rose and went out laughing, and we were able to take some rest, under protection of the commandant, who remained with us. I have no idea how long we waited before the train started. I remember that it was a long time. But my patient was peacefully reposing, and that was all I cared about. At length the apparently interminable line of cars—the two ends were seldom visible at the same time—got under way and went on, sometimes at such a rate that I fully expected we should run off the line, and at other times crawling along at a snail's pace. In the fresh morning light the country was radiantly lovely, and the straggling columns of Boer riders that we overtook from time to time animated the landscape, and gave it a rare and special character of its own, that would have delighted any seeker after sharp impressions.

Whenever we came up with any of these horsemen there was an interchange of wild cheering and waving of hats between them and their brethren in the train. Why? I did not understand at the time, I do not understand now, and I never shall.

We reached Pretoria next morning. I was so frightfully black from head to foot that my dear friends and compatriots, who took me into their home whenever I came, broke into loud laughter as soon as they saw me, and declared that I must certainly have travelled on the engine and helped to stoke it. I was not presentable until forty-eight hours afterwards.

To briefly summarize what remains to be told, I continued to nurse Colonel Maximoff. His wounds were slow to heal, and as I told him after my first inspection of them, proved so severe as to prevent him from taking any further part in the campaign. He was thus compelled, much against his will, to give up. I could relate many interesting incidents and execute sketches that would represent certain Boer personages in a far from flattering light; but as Colonel Maximoff's sister of charity (his own expression), and sometimes his secretary, my conscience compels me to observe the strictest secrecy.

I was still at Pretoria when, on the 14th of May, I received a telegram from Europe announcing a loss which necessitated my returning home. I took the Messageries Maritimes' steamer *Iraouaddy* at Lorenzo Marquez, and landed at Marseilles on the 28th of June. I had left Europe on the 25th of November with my heart full of pity and sisterly love for the Boers. I returned home depressed and heartsick. My eyes were opened. My readers will realise that this destruction of my faith, my beliefs, and my delusions, noble and humanitarian as they were, was indescribably painful to me.

www.ingramcontent.com/pod-product-compliance
Lightning Source LLC
Chambersburg PA
CBHW031901090426
42741CB00005B/597